A Brief History of Fear

The Relative World Belief – III

POWERFUL NEW TEACHINGS FROM

"A COURSE IN MIRACLES"

Sharon Moriarty

GATEWAY TO ETERNITY PUBLICATIONS

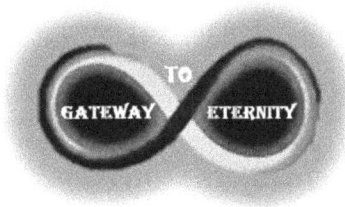

http://www.GatewayToEternity.com

A Brief History of Fear

PREFACE

Life is short! We have but an infinitesimal slice of sidereal time in which to live it up, bask in the glory and extract all the pleasure and meaning we can from life. The salt shaker moves in only one direction, and it is always running low. Your life energy is readily dispersing, even as you read this and dropping into the void. Existence holds still for no one. You may be wondering why you should bother to read a book about fear. After all, isn't life such a miserable affair all on its own? Why dare then to open Pandora's box and release a tirade of fearful and demonic thoughts, to wreak havoc on your mind? You probably already have enough crap in your life. Why introduce new sources of interference into that convoluted mess? Your day-to-day existence is so full of vicious cycles, deadening patterns, and unseemly contradictions and from every angle, the never-ending wails of insanity and restless discontent scream out from every orifice! Aren't happiness, love, and meaning what is worth striving for the most!

My first thought on writing this was, "*Hopefully; I am not going to end up stringing myself before I am ready to complete it.*" It was sure that this new enterprise was going to take me on a downer and perhaps, even become the blue-print for my destruction. Still, these reactions were puzzling to me, and I had to wonder, from where inside they were bubbling up. What part of my being trembled so extensively at the very prospect of taking fear head-on? I was about to abandon the project, except this very compelling thought, kept popping into my head "*Those who do not understand fear become controlled by it.*" Our subjugation by fear is inevitable whether we are conscious of it or not because fear grows in darkness and is vanquished only by light. Like ostriches, we like to dig our heads in the sand at times, and there is nothing wrong with that. The overload we face in life can often be excessive! Even so, no one genuinely believes that sickness or cancer is going to disappear simply by ignoring it, just as no one expects to become rich without persevering, making strategic investments and capitalizing on ideas.

Our world is more an uninspired ideational wasteland than a magical kingdom. We live predominantly in a realm powered out of our insecurities, desires, and fears and these determine the scope of our freedom and joy. What we do not face, or integrate becomes denied and is rapidly dismissed from our active awareness. All this hidden activity empowers fear to thrive, to become Master over our roost. Licensed with all the crippling energy of our mind and thought, it then dictates what we will do and what we will seek to avoid.

THE POWER OF NEGATIVE THINKING

When Norman Vincent Peale first released his profound insights in the book titled *"The Power of Positive Thinking*," it swiftly became an overnight sensation. People were attracted to it, like moths to the flame. Bliss bunnies from all around emerged from their private worldly cubbyholes wanting to immerse themselves completely in its positive energy and illuminating thought. They aspired to surround themselves with Avatars, Angelic beings and the forces of light and they believed anything was possible, once one planted the right seeds. Yes, the universe is overflowing with creative energy and all things are theoretically possible. Why then do we find our appetites, lusts, passions, and cravings not instantly fulfilled and our dreams shattered before they have a chance to blossom? Why do we become so easily disenchanted, depressed, derailed and unhinged? Why do many fall into dark pits of despair from which they never recover? After all, if the formula is so simple to apply, its results should be abundantly evident. There must be another side to this existential and spiritual equation which we are conveniently ignoring. One just as powerful, if not more so!

Probing a little closer, we find that bliss bunnies only emphasize one side of the coin—the **"Heads"** side. They conveniently ignore the inescapable verity that every "*Heads*" must come with its "***Tails***." They deliberately and witlessly avoid the abiding realization that the forces of negativity, chaos, boredom, and fear are just as powerful as the positive, loving and creative energies in the universe. Their strong aversion, to this incontestable insight, places them in a state of denial, and their rejection of certain aspects of our divine will and mind-power exacts a tremendous cost. Since the denied becomes all-powerful, the sword of creativity soon becomes blunt and inefficacious. As one begins to attract mixed results, they start to lose interest. Then the fountain of inspiration dries up, and the potential for entering highly imaginative, visionary and creative states wanes. Undoubtedly, when we squash and repress unwelcome thoughts and feelings deep in our subconscious, this does not mitigate and eliminate their dark energy. In fact, they become all the more formidable, for our doing so. What flourishes in our unconscious is highly potent in its effects and continues to exercise its influence on all our thoughts, emotions, actions and behaviors. All that becomes lost through denial is our power and mastery over what we deny.

Norman Vincent Peale only delivered half the equation. He should have immediately followed it up with a book titled *"The Power of Negative Thinking."* Isn't it so that those getting ready to be beheaded by their ISIS Captors never thought they would be in this predicament! Maybe, if they had been a little more cautious and mistrustful, they would not be kneeling now in the sand with the blade pressed firmly against their necks. Finding all these human mosquitoes and cockroaches behind them getting ready to suck on their blood for the media. Perhaps if they had been a little less *gung-ho,* less buoyed by the Myth of their indestructibility, this would not be happening. They could have been relaxing in the comfort of their living room recliners smoking the hookah and knocking back a cold one. Sadly, they could not stop flapping their beaks and believed they were invincible. Hence, they never indemnified themselves against lunatics and extremely risk-filled situations. Instead, floating about on their wings of optimism and incurable delight, they projected commendable motives, unwavering trust and positive expectations to all. All of which conditioned them to be abundantly naïve, vulnerable and blind to the faces of evil, emptiness, and savagery lurking in humanity.

In this arena, negative thinking patterns and defensive behaviors arrive as our rescuers. They embody wisdom
which insulates us from nasty circumstances and can even
save our lives on occasion. No doubt, we owe an enormous
debt to our cynicism and negativity. Excessive positivity
and inordinate optimism, on the other hand, are often
highly destructive to our well-being. Our confidence and
cocksure attitudes will not protect us and often do us great
harm. Positive intentions can function as lethal poisons,
and be turned into weapons, against us. There are myriad
insidious ideologies that seep into our consciousness
which coerce us into being overly gullible and credulous.
Often, we imprudently let our shields down to welcome in
all Trojans Horses and gifts that are attractive only at the
surface.

The enduring power of our negativity is swept under the
carpet, far too often. Reflect for a moment on all the broken relationships, destroyed marriages and financial disasters you could have averted were there just an ounce of
negative thinking there to balance the wheels! How many
times, for instance, have you not thought in a moment of
epiphanic ideation "*I wish I had never brought that subject
up*" or "*What got over me! I wish I had not done that!*" Nevertheless, amped up, under the hypnotizing spell of new-

found enthusiasm, we make unrealistic promises and take on tremendous risks that will just burn us up. How many CEOs of startups have agonized and become bitter on seeing all their energy and ingenuity failing to make a mark? Many have watched powerlessly while all their free time, life-savings and most cherished aspirations became ravenously consumed by the insatiable beast of their pet enterprise or passion!

THE PRACTICAL BENEFITS OF NEGATIVE THINKING

Unless you reap immense practical benefits from your negative thinking strategies, you will be unlikely to engage them in transforming your life. Being unable to leverage their full power, you will remain incapacitated. Living with excessive uncensored optimism is like trying to fly successfully through life on just one wing. You will remain unbalanced and disharmonious and unable to function efficiently and with grace. There are some basic principles associated with negative thinking that you can immediately put to work for your benefit. Below I enumerate a few. I will now delve into these in some detail:

1. Cynicism is a Powerful Tool

2. Test People on Small Things.

3. Don't Take Anybody's Word or Past Experience as Golden.

4. Excessive Optimism Leads to Rapid Failure

5. Hone the Power of your Instincts and Intuition

6. Belittle Your Mind-Power at your own Risk

7. Know that True Love is a Myth

CYNICISM IS A POWERFUL TOOL

"The power of accurate observation is commonly called cynicism by those who have not got it."

[George Bernard Shaw]

Cynicism is perceived socially as a somewhat tasteless if not revolting garment to wear. Many conceive it as some mental virus from which they steer well away. Nothing could be further from the truth. In contrast, cynicism is like a badge of honor, that can only be worn by those who have truly lived and taken risks. One who knows the dangers and has learned from past failures is likely to be more cautious and cynical. It is not by accident that the older we get, the more we mature into regular incorrigible cynics; young folk, conversely, tend to be hopeless idealists. Generically speaking, **Age is Wisdom**! The wisdom gained from living in the trenches and overcoming many challenging obstacles in life. Of course, there are always exceptions! Some remain naïve, puerile and overly trusting as they advance in years; this just signifies that they have been overly pampered, socially insulated or else parasitically lived off the efforts of others.

Not all forms of cynicism are beneficial to our health and advancement. Some can be toxic and detrimental to our progress. Lamentably, we oversimplify and lump all types of cynicism under the same banner—that of the skull and crossbones. There are two fundamentals breeds of cynicism, namely: **(1) Corrosive Cynicism** and **(2) Progressive cynicism**

Corrosive Cynicism:

This form of cynicism aims at knocking every endeavor and submerging all in the subaqueous swamp of perennial ignorance. Whenever you feel invisible forces dampening your prospects of advancement, you are possibly surrounded by a nest of caustic cynics. There is a vicious cauldron of human parasites who delight in sucking the wind out from the sails of every progressive venture. Some will sabotage every effort you make to live up to your potential. Their ingrained notions of inferiority and fears of abandonment motivate them to dethrone others. They love to engage in toxic relationships of dependency and play various guilt games to lure you in and trap you. Alternatively, they will overwhelm by implanting unconscious negative suggestions. The subliminal influence this exerts over the years can be enormous. There can be irreparable long-term damage inflicted on your psyche.

Direct family members are often the worst enemy in thwarting your ambitions. They assume the right and privilege to put their siblings down, the instant the mood takes them. Controlling corporations, too, are an unrecognized evil. They instantiate measures to subjugate and subordinate their staff so they can proceed unhindered to make unrealistic demands and have each work 24x7. They aim to destroy your confidence and self-esteem, and overall trust in your abilities to succeed on your own. The incessant stream of reprimands and clipping of wings can leave you rigor mortis in your prime. Meanwhile, any dissenting employee is speedily branded as "pigheaded and incapable of teamwork." Then either fired or put in a cage for careful observation.

Progressive Cynicism:

Progressive cynicism has nothing to do with callously taking another down or sabotaging plans or initiatives which promise a great benefit. Instead, it seeks to uncover the unseen flaws in any strategy, action or endeavor and nips these in the bud to save great pain and cost downstream. It shines a beneficial light on the chronic mistakes of others so that they can overcome their blind spots and blossom to their full potential. Often, the one thing we expressly needed to hear, no one is brave enough to tell us, and we remain crippled until an incurable cynic crosses into our path.

In the business world, progressive cynicism is vital for Risk Management. It helps safeguard an enterprise, and ensures that is not blinded by overly-simplistic projections. In any given plan, there are always hidden variables that can become dominant and direct to progress or failure. Likewise, many "known" variables are overly optimistic, and they leave no room for fluctuation, outliers or contingencies. Statisticians and Actuaries, for example, build their models based on the testimony of historical data. They extrapolate this information into the future, to determine potential risk and exposure. However such models are incredibly static and do not account for a changing world and fluctuating moods in the marketplace. Events are happening now that can entirely redirect the outcome. The butterfly effect is very real in finance and economics. Tiny parametric variations and random events, not deemed statistically

significant in the present can yet exert a prodigious influence in the near future. Such events and anomalies are
mostly dismissed because they cannot be included in the
complex models developed. The 2008 stock market crash
which led to the global recession is a classic example of the
failures in economic and financial modeling.

TEST PEOPLE ON SMALL THINGS

From the cradle to the grave, we are all sold a crock of BS on the merit gained from developing various virtues and codes of conduct. For example, we are taught to be more trusting of others and with life in general. Expected to blindly trust strangers, large corporations, the wealthy, unstable governments, fickle politicians, and healthcare companies, etc. Extending trust without question is a dangerous pursuit, and it leaves us with an enormous blind spot. Unless everyone is considered suspect from the beginning, one will soon be the patsy. Common sense dictates, we should never put all our eggs in one basket or trust any person or enterprise whose motives may be dubious, distorted, deceptive or malicious from the beginning.

A basic maxim of life is that "*Each will attempt to take or do whatever they can get away with.*" Another piece of sagacious advice is "*Trust No One, on instinct*!" Of course, these maxims are not true of everyone, but they should certainly feed one's decisions. Predacious actions and behaviors tend to become more magnified and reckless the more powerful an enterprise is. Corporations and governments are at the top of this hierarchy. Even friends of a lifetime will abandon you in a flash when you no longer serve their best interests or long-term goals. Certainly, it is a hard truth to face, but in the final analysis, the world is a carnivorous jungle

A while back, I worked for this startup in Silicon Valley. One day a coworker, I managed, came in with a pissed attitude and positively needed to vent but was repressing it. Since he was a genial and stable guy; this new attitude caught me a little off-guard. I was aware that he had been recently married and had a newborn on the way. Finally, I invited him out to lunch and asked: "*What's up?*" He related how he had been declined on a home mortgage application that morning. Since he was a dependable guy with excellent credit and a good salary, it was hard to understand. It turned out that his credit wasn't the issue. He got rejected because a friend with poor credit had badgered him into cosigning on his home loan two years prior. This friend had taken advantage of their friendship, and now he was finding it impossible to procure a home loan for himself. His blanket trust in others had cost him dearly, and they weren't even friends anymore. I commiserated with him and said: "*It always pays to think small. You should test people first on small amounts and on accomplishing trivial tasks before placing enormous faith in their goodwill and accountability."*

In life, we find that certain people have commendable integrity, and others most certainly do not. Some speak only the truth, and others are duplicitous creatures that merchandise in nothing but deceptions, two-faced trickery, and lies. Once you lose your integrity, you can never get it back. Those who readily cave on small things soon find it easier to sell themselves for even larger gifts. Rapidly they morph into immensely fraudulent double-dealing beings who are masters of pretense, dissimulation, and endless equivocation. This reminds me of an old joke: "This extremely well-dressed, albeit seedy looking old man comes up to an attractive woman in a bar and asks: '*Would you sleep with me for a million dollars?*' The woman ponders over it for a moment and answers '*Yes!*' The man then asks: '*Would you sleep with me for ten dollars?*' The woman is mortified and immediately responds: '*Of course not! What do you think I am?*' To this, the old man slyly responds: '*We have already established what you are! We are now just haggling over your price!*'

Don't Take Anyone's Word or Past Experience as Golden

"The reasonable man adapts himself to the world; the unreasonable one persists in trying to adapt the world to himself. Therefore, all progress depends on the unreasonable man."

[George Bernard Shaw]

Most of us are creatures of habit. We prefer the known over the unknown, and tend to align ourselves only with those who echo our views and beliefs. Our natural instinct is to cringe whenever we are driven into unfamiliar territory or are forced to embrace new situations, ideas or technologies. Presently there is a profusion of dark forces at play in the world, that keep us hostage to fear. So we continuously worry about how we are going to protect our livelihoods, life savings, health, privacy, etc. The suspect list also includes everything from

GMOs and pesticides in our food, and endless drug pushing by the medical community to Cyberfraud, Automation, Self-driving cars, miniaturized tracking devices, nanotechnology bots, etc. All the same, no corporate empire, revolutionizing invention, or pioneering change ever originated from those who merely photocopied the voice and opinion of the majority. Can you even imagine the extensive loss to civilization had Tesla simply agreed with Edison's view that *'DC is the only way to go in Electrical Distribution.'* Notable figures like Tesla, Galileo, Columbus, Einstein, Newton, Mahatma Gandhi, Jesus Christ, etc. became influential catalysts for far-reaching change because they were courageous enough to dissent with popular opinions. Collectively, they triggered radical and progressive evolutions in our world.

99% or more of the general population will never enjoy a truly original thought of their own. Most are suckers for whatever is craftily disseminated by the Media channels. The lion's share mindlessly absorbs any poisonous agenda or program of indoctrination directed their way. Through blindly and imprudently embracing misinformation we collude in reinforcing severely distorted messages. Our minds are like wet sponges left soaking in the vapid pools of mediocrity and we are always in a readiness state for brainwashing. We are highly uncritical of all nonsense propaganda propagated by the misinformation conduits of modern day technology. Our neural pathways have long been bombarded and fried with numerous blueprints for social conditioning. Likewise, our unconscious mental processes ravenously devour whatever the external environment pipes into the subliminal and supraliminal channels of our awareness. If you want to know what the ocean is, you would not ask a fish because the fish has never been apart from the ocean. Similarly, it is unwise to esteem the arbitrary opinions of the herd. Anyone who has never gone against the grain or followed their visceral instincts and intuition is unlikely to be a harbinger of future progress.

The simple verity is that sixty-six million French people can be wrong. This incontrovertible fact has been proven countless times in world history. How many peered up at the Sun and believed it to be circling the earth until Galileo said otherwise? How many still believe to this day that their bodies genuinely exist while their minds are ephemeral quantities? How few have detected the sublime and superconscious realms just beyond the mundane one witnessed through our senses? When Steve Jobs introduced the first iPods and iPhones, he had not invented anything new. He merely had taken existing technologies and combined them on a single platform that was more compact and aesthetic. Nonetheless, how many hundreds of millions knew these technologies intimately and did not see this opportunity? They missed the opportunity because the limitless landscape of unseen potentiality became subsumed by their conditioned belief and vision of what was possible. We are hypnotized and fooled by the world of appearances and cannot see past the dim offerings presented at the surface because of our extreme limitations. We perceive through our internal mental constructs, and these, in turn, emerge from the beliefs and opinions that shape us. Only when we begin to think differently, will we perceive differently because the world crystallizes from our beliefs.

The Art of Negative Thinking is a highly constructive pursuit since it leads to Self-Liberation. It involves never accepting second-hand opinion in place of first-hand knowledge and immediate experience. We are wise only to the extent that we know ourselves. Unless we interrogate all our premises and beliefs most rigorously and test their veracity for ourselves, we cannot claim to know something. Some of the tools, needed for our success include reason, intuition, self-knowledge, and experience.

Intellectual knowledge and words can only take one so far. In the final analysis, unless a knowledge has been verified viscerally at one's core, it remains conjecture, and it will not transform and revolutionize one's life. It is just like empty symbols arbitrarily scribbled on the ocean.

EXCESSIVE OPTIMISM LEADS TO RAPID FAILURE

The optimist lives perennially in a bubble. This bubble is his fantasyland where he can safely daydream about future success without any danger of intrusion. He ignores critical elements in the fuller picture and welcomes only those who share in his fantasies and beliefs. In this reality distortion field, only positive reinforcement of private delusions is allowed. Candid, impartial and honest opinions become brutally suppressed when they do not reinforce the dominant script of our chief protagonist. They become conceived as a voice of negativity that needs to be drowned out and promptly hushed. Over time, all invitees learn to shut their mouths until that fatal day when the bubble finally goes splash.

Collectively, this bubble universe is all around us. We witness it in the stock market, financial sector, real estate and healthcare. It is rampant in most Tech and Biogenetic corporations. Whenever pharmaceutical costs are allowed to escalate uncontrollably, or wherever overt reality is stubbornly denied, bubble power is at work. We have all got a hint of it at times, usually when projections of success seemly highly inflated and too good to be true. Everyone seems to have bought into the conspiracy and is playing the game. I have experienced it many times working for startups. Watched glitzy marketing personnel running around with their laptops presenting illustrious slides predicting where corporate profits will be a year, five years and ten years down the line. Then a few weeks later, I arrive at the office to find that an entire product area and development team needed to be canned overnight. Sometimes, we catch its scent when a large corporation becomes insolvent, and the stock price plummets. Soon all high-end equipment becomes auctioned off for pennies, and stunned employees start googling the EDD and Cobra websites or advertising a garage sale.

After a while, we begin to feel that we may have better luck scrying into a crystal ball than trusting market projections and analysts opinions. Since all vested interests are unduly buoyed by excessive optimism, they cannot provide an impartial outlook. High-level managers tune out and turn a deaf ear once they hear any talk of building in contingency plans to guard against uncertainties or project delays. Any hint of there being additional costs, limited marketability or insufficient resource estimates is tantamount to being seditious. Merely proposing the implementation of pilot studies with limited feature sets is deemed to be unwarranted. Nevertheless, all these factors are what eventually bring the beast of excessive optimism in industry to its knees.

Optimism is neither a bad nor a good attribute, in itself. It all depends on how it is substantiated and what are the grounding forces that contain it. When it turns deaf and blind, it becomes dangerous. Overly optimistic forecasts need to be held in check and counterbalanced by the forces of realism. There should be the expectation that many unknown variables and uncertainties will influence the final result. Such parameters can include changing customer buying patterns, unforeseen competitors, new information, systemic flaws, extreme environmental conditions emerging, political instabilities and so forth. Injecting a good dose of pessimism early on can save a corporation billions. It intercepts and restrains the spreading of starry-eyed guesstimates to others. Silencing the voice of all skeptics and cynics and sending them off to the slaughterhouse is the sure path to failure. Instead, they should be embraced and valued for taking a neutral and far more encompassing stance.

HONE THE POWER OF YOUR INSTINCTS AND INTUITION.

The Art of Negative thinking treasures all approaches that are holistic, and paradigm shifting and all which rises about the shallow obscuring mists of pure intellection. Often the crucial information, needed for making a decision is not out there in the data, conjectures, projections, or reasoned analysis but it lies deep inside ourselves. Our zealous focus on externals has caused us to lose sight of the fountain of wisdom that exists within. We see and interpret our world through many eyes, at once. The eyes of our intellect and emotion; fears and lusts; senses and conceptual evolutionary capacities. Most importantly, we have the power to view the world through the Vision of Spirit and its limitless Knowledge. This world of our perception can only tell us so much since it solely reflects who we Are at the surface. All great inventions, flashes of insight, creative urges, and innovational decisions are inspired from far beyond the pale of our conscious awareness.

At many junctures in life, it is critical to know when to bale. We must assess our position fearlessly and from all our perspectives at once. The optimal time will be different for everyone, and only you can assess your unique situation. It has never been about convincing others but only yourself. You may, for instance, be working for a company that is unreasonable or inordinately demanding. This toxic environment may be crushing your spirit or placing you under psychological attack. It may, for example, be replete with ambitious youngsters who are eager to please and ready to sacrifice their wellbeing for the corporate interests. Such can-do, compliant folk get leveraged and burned-out all the time. Your intellect may be screaming "**Stay!**" and indicating that it is sheer madness to leave without an alternative or backup plan. All the same, your instinct and intuition have voices too!. Your instinct is screaming into your emotions and viscera, and your intuition feeds from the wisdom of Spirit. To discount such voices and listen only to that of your intellect may result in chronic health problems, self-hatred or even suicide further down the road.

Negative thinking rises above the ordinary dimensions of life. It explores other vistas pivotal for maintaining ongoing happiness and health. It says to the intellect "*I have heard all your nonsense and acted upon it for years and still I am miserable. Give me something more or else shut-up!*"

BELITTLE YOUR MIND-POWER AT YOUR OWN RISK

Thought can be both creative and miscreative. New Age thinking focuses predominantly on the creative aspect. No one doubts that our positive intentions can be extremely potent and contagious in their effects. Our sincerely held hopes can rapidly turn the universe on its side and lead to the miraculous. Undreamed of changes can instantaneously occur which catapult us into the stratosphere of higher knowledge. Changes which raise us high above the melting pot of the unseemly humdrum existence. Our untaintable will can brush past all illusions; accelerate our future and trigger a quantum leap in our spiritual evolution.

Nonetheless, this potency is rendered unproductive unless we embrace the incontrovertible knowledge that: **(1) All thought is life** and **(2) Thought is holistic in its essence**. A single thought readily cross-pollinates to other domains of thought and experience. Thus it shapes our worldview and influences the unique identities, we adopt. When we seek to avoid unpleasant thoughts, we silently empower a vast network of fears to fester and grow because each fear thought is seamlessly connected to many others. All share the same underlying content.

The enemy of positivity is not negativity nor is pessimism the enemy of optimism. Viewed wisely and perspicaciously both aspects are understood to be mutually co-creative since they exist in a dualistic relationship. The real enemy of positivity is negative thoughts that have been repressed and denied and not included in the overall equation. Such negative thoughts hold tremendous power and traction, and they thrive even more when denied. Their effects will rise to impede one's progress and soon darken the entire picture. Such is the cost of denial. Finding your creative intentions dampened and accomplishing nothing; you will become quickly frustrated and just give up.

The trick is to embrace negativity in the right measure and at the right time. Just as a poison can be used to cure and a vaccine is formed from harmful bacteria or viruses that have been neutralized, so it is with negativity. It is only toxic if administered at the wrong dosage at an inopportune time. Negativity is not here to cripple and derail but to keep us realistic, balanced and sane. It can readily transform impractical, half-baked ideas into living possibilities which then flourish on their intrinsic merit. It can trim and discard all which is unnecessary or redundant, so saving countless energy expenditures.

Ultimately, one who embraces negativity and cynicism in the right measure enjoys a happier, more progressive, realistic and stable life. Only one who knows how to balance the energies of positivity and negativity rightly can be sane. Of course, such mastery is an art in itself.

Negativity has nothing to do with endorsing defeatist behaviors and oxygen deprived mindsets. Its focus is on recognizing and balancing our thoughts and probing deeply into all aspects of a situation, even those we are averse to. This automatically levels the playing field, and it establishes a rock-solid foundation for making wise and judicious decisions. Whenever you disavow your Mind-power and the tremendous influence your negative thoughts exact on your life and perception, you do so at your own risk. Over time you will feel prey to all thought energy you failed to acknowledge. The demons of your underworld and subconscious mind will roam whether you admit they are present or not. Denied, you are simply living in a hot-air balloon and a life of delusion.

KNOW THAT TRUE LOVE IS A MYTH

Love relationships are like storefronts. The best aspects are presented in display cases on the outside and used as bait to attract another. Do not be surprised later if you have been hooked and baited by an Anti-Christ. Everyone has their vices and demons; so don't be fooled by superficial appearances and a glamorous façade. Negative thinking strategies caution you not to fall into this trap. It teaches the sooner you find out the core nature of another; the better it will be for you. You would not buy a product until you first knew all its features, capabilities, usefulness and price. So why would you fall hook, line, and sinker into a relationship and start flattering another without knowing all their benefits, and flaws, practicality and cost?

It is unwise to surrender all your trust and faith until the object of your affection has shown they are somehow worthy of it. Love is a bubble, like many others. This bubble is constructed from all your narcissistic tendencies projected to another or as Freud called it, 'an aberration of self-love.' The illusionary paradise inside this bubble is not real but a mirage of the mind that will soon let you down. Striving for unconditional Love is truly a noble goal but ultimately unachievable wherever any hint of fear persists. Fear is unavoidable in this world, so all loving relationships remain a bartering of illusions. Fear makes one contractive, rather than expansive to life, and it bars unconditional Love from your awareness.

Denying your fear feelings is not going to blaze a pathway towards your release. Unless you are willing to vigilantly pursue the roots of your fears and shine them away under the light of spiritual vision, nothing fundamental will change for you. The purpose of this book is to accomplish such a task. It will expose the real roots of your fear in the hopes that you will no longer avoid what is stifling your life energy and potential. Only so, can you awaken! Until you are ready to descend past all the fear clouds, you will not find the light within that is inextinguishable and the Source of all Bliss.

The human mind tends to focus on specifics, and so it is with fear. The important recognition is sagaciously discerning that all fear is metaphysical in its essence and its source lies far deeper than the world we perceive. Exploring fear's ontological basis and all dark cornerstones which support it is the primary focus of this book. Rightly interpreted then, this teaching is one of healing since it aims to remove all obstacles to Love. Once you disband all such impediments, the Truth within will radiate outward into your perception vaporizing all last holdouts of fear. Then the gates of the eternal paradise will swing open and transport you to Enlightenment and Unassailable Peace!

LEARN TO HARNESS YOUR FEARS

F ear, like negativity, has received a bad rap. Nonetheless, most aspects of life are found to have a gainful, productive, and salubrious purpose once interpreted wisely. Otherwise, this situation or event would not be appearing in our perception and thought-streams. Fear, too, has a valuable and laudable purpose. It can stimulate us into becoming more courageous and adventurous in spirit. The friction it offers can enable us to overcome vast corrosive formations and skeletons in our psyche that are hampering and plaguing our life. Rising above such steep, arduous terrain, we heal and come to a new awareness of ourselves.

The presence of fear serves as a very cogent and persuasive reflection; one that reminds how we are investing too much with the ego and its self-destructive ways. This hellish reflection lucidly depicts how far we have wandered from the ways of Love. Fear arises whenever we indulge too extensively in the unreal and cherish foolish fantasies in place of Truth. Thankfully, all wrong decisions can be corrected, once reinterpreted sanely under the right light. From the higher vantage point, all rationalizations, justifications, and misinterpretations serving to protect fear are isolated and dismantled.

In this teaching, I will lay bare the real roots of fear so that the pure light of Creation can be restored. This unveiling liberates and empowers, and it enables one to sip from the cup of unvanquishable peace, bliss, and authentic Love. I will also investigate the dominant mechanisms by which fear survives and propagates in mind, and review the misplaced beliefs, attractions, and defenses which serve to promote it. I will scrutinize all ego compensations and idols that aim to screen our underlying fear from conscious awareness. Since all ego gifts are woven from the fabric of illusions, they can never succeed in bringing any lasting cure or Salvation.

This teaching gives you the mental tools by which to escape fear and heal your life. I am not here to babysit you or to go over specific concerns. Instead, I will present some case histories and anecdotes that may prove pivotal and illuminating. The ultimate goal is for you to become self-liberating. Once you become proficient at self-analysis and introspection and able to discern the common elements underscoring your particular fears, you will competently relinquish each with ease. After all, to feed a man, a fish is to feed him for a day, but to teach a man to fish is to feed him for life.

Once you have penetrated to the core of your fears and know with certitude that though in form they appear different, in content, they remain the same, you will have reached a higher plateau in your spiritual and metaphysical understanding. All arise from spiritual contraction and an underlying lovelessness that alienates your being. Our goal is to journey past all fear clouds that have held you, hostage, for far too long. You will be freed from a great burden once you can efficiently uncover and uproot all fear-based maneuverings of the ego and avoid all its allurements and temptations. On this Holy journey, you will become unburdened, altruistic and forgiving and more open, expansive and adventurous in life. Finally, cured of all self-destructive tendencies and wrong-minded beliefs, you will find the Holy Grail at the core of Life and drink from that limitless fountain of unconditional Love, in which your original Self is always blissfully immersed.

PEERING BEYOND THE MASK

In our progression, through the minefield of life, various epiphanies and truisms dawn to our conscious awareness. At times, we experience synchronicities or capture a glimpse of the higher picture. Such revelations only emerge, at the moment we are ripe. We instinctively fight against the new understandings because they demand change or seem to inflict a temporary loss of power or command. Nonetheless, the message communicated is irrefutable, unambiguous and lucid, and it illuminates beyond words or worlds.

For instance, you may have ascertained by now, that this Relative World, continuously pressures us into operating as two-faced beings. We live in a very fake and superficial cauldron of senseless activity, and existence wages a full-out war against all who would retain the crown jewels of their integrity and pride. It aims to ridicule, sabotage, terrify and decimate us at every juncture and it aspires to humiliate and humble us. It demands we put on masks and function as aliens to ourselves. The quiet voice of our inner guidance is easily drowned out by the mindless ranting and hysteria of the masses, as by that hive of immense hyperactivity that surrounds us. Our authentic natures we profoundly repress when they do not correlate with what society currently sanctions or upholds. From the get-go, we learn to become opportunistic and chameleon-like. We feel coerced into chopping off a new piece of ourselves every day, and thus we soon find ourselves living a deception! We have one face we proudly display to others and another we keep well hidden away.

Our public disguise often endows us with great pride. It presents a radiant and glowing image to the gallery of humanity of our compassion, innocence, altruism, and power. This stunning portrait omits no detail, however insignificant, that may augment us further in the eyes of others. Our spirit of adventure, daring, and innovation, is all there, along with a portrayal of our complete immunity to the ills of the world. On the canvas is engraved, the golden silhouette of an invulnerable and conscientious being which the world is powerless to defile, subvert or overpower. Yes, we like to think of ourselves as pure lotuses living far above the mud of this worldly swamp. Reigning as exalted beings, safely sealed off from the animal arena all around us.

Even so, beneath the mask of our perfect composure lies another. One we never dare present to others, as we mosey about in the metropolitan circus of the known universe. One we are so deeply ashamed of that we even keep it concealed from our conscious awareness. It pictures a fearful, trembling creature, ridden with various anxieties and paralyzed with the pain of guilt. One of a hurt, and torn child who cannot comprehend anything, he perceives. This infant sees truly and branded into his heart is the terrifying reflection of a world that is loveless, merciless, self-absorbed, directionless and conflicted. A capricious world, brimming with unquenchable hate and never-ending want.

There is an unspoken truth, we rarely hear. Only in moments of self-honesty will we hear that gentle whispering in our ears, of a message both quiet and certain. One that confidently declares that "*It is impossible to be in this world and not be without fear.*" As long as we believe we are in the world, fear will continue to poison our minds and shape our decisions. It will sink its teeth deep into our bones and transform us into vile creatures that we will no longer recognize. In our intensely disconnected and emotionally frozen state, we often lash out mercilessly and attack without provocation. Often we will maliciously destroy another's reputation, if only to rise a little higher in the pack. Character assassinations are everywhere on psycho-planet, and the media outlets perennially live off the smell of fresh meat. Every day, there is another juicy story of some celebrity, we eagerly besmirch because we love to smear the free riders with our brush of insidious darkness.

Henry Miller considered his hero, as one who had conquered all his fears. He presented the very portrait of a living immortal, forever ready to face the harsh truths of his or her naked existence, upfront and personal with no unnecessary frills, or deceptions. One willing to chew on the bones of their pain and suffering and ready to suck it in intravenously, if necessary, if it could extend some additional life or wisdom. His hero was no escapist seeking to cover the unsightly with fanciful imaginations and dense clouds of denial. Miller's hero, though noble in intent, seems a tragic figure when dissected and post-analyzed. A pre-programmed puppet on strings, ready to charge out and tilt at the many nightmarish windmills of terror, continuously besieging his senses. One willing to embrace all without regret or fear and yet with no end purpose in sight.

A noble and worthwhile mission must have some higher purpose, or it remains just an idle misadventure. One taken by frivolous beings, who have time to recklessly squander. It should be grasped, from the outset that any attempt to master or conquer fear which precludes uncovering divine wisdom is an entire waste of time. Unmasking the perfect knowledge that exists within is the only way to shine away unrealities. Thus one arrives at the Source of unconditional Love which casts out all fear! A hero may be willing to face their fears, but they are helpless to overcome them, without wisdom. Nonetheless, since the hero never empowers fear to thread its way deep underground, its destructive power is held in check. His acknowledgment of them guarantees that they will not become sublimated and unconscious. It is evident that the causes of our fear are as numerous as the grains of sand that lie along the Ganges. However, on closer examination, it becomes apparent that the bulk of our fears can be quantized into certain distinct categories, as illustrated in the diagram below.

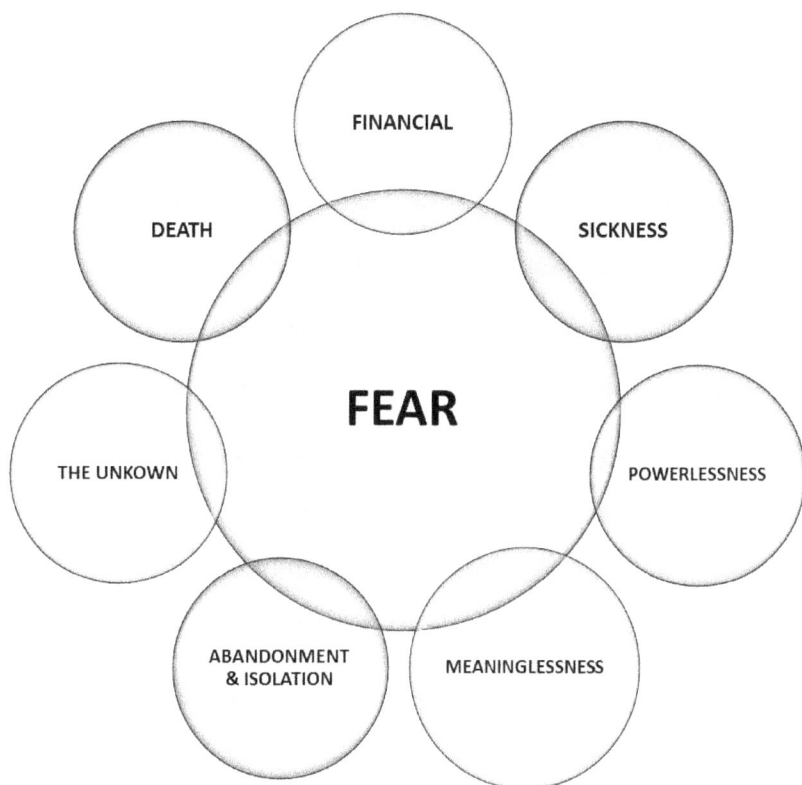

OUR BASIC FEAR TYPES

In Part II of this series, "*The Myth of Separation,*" I explored thoroughly the problems associated with living in a body and inhabiting this dream universe of separation. Since our "separated" condition is a projected illusion, all our fears ultimately arise from identifying with an unreal frame-work. Within this bleak artifice of a space-time existence, we feel vulnerable and frail and therefore willingly lend our ears to the voice of separation, namely the ego. Our fears derive from endorsing toxic egoistic thinking strategies which are highly destructive in their makeup. Once these miscreative thought processes are exposed and abandoned, fear is no more.

In this transmission, we will engage in a relentless campaign to eviscerate all dark thinking patterns which fear continuously promotes and hides behind. Fear's essential nature will be investigated and probed from many lustrous and unique vantage points. We will demystify the gifts of the ego and explore how they encapsulate an offering of fear and death, at their core. We are easily deceived because all such trinkets come in a beautiful package; one our minds find so alluring, even hypnotizing. It will become increasingly evident that our fears and insecurities ultimately arise from living through the fractured identity, known in Course vernacular as *Split-Mind*. The projected counterpart of which is this hallucinatory luniverse, known as *the Relative World*.

You will undertake a daring and inspirational adventure, (not dissimilar to ones taken in the past by the Knights Templar,) towards the real roots of your fear. Voyaging rapidly past the illusory skin-deep domains, you will enter the heart of the subaqueous realms of mind. Finally, the natural illumination of eternal spirit will shine away all deceptions and false thought-forms that have beclouded you for many past eons So do you become liberated from your self-made prison-house of darkness, and fully healed! Restored to the perfect Love of Creation which fear had always obfuscated! The diagram below depicts fear's place and role in perpetuating the Relative World Cycle.

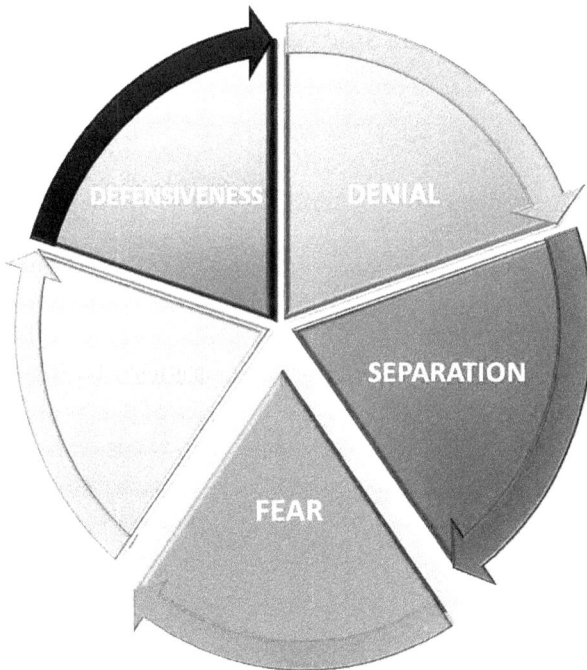

HOW FEAR FITS INTO THE CAUSE-AND-EFFECT CYCLE THAT PERPETU-ATES THE RELATIVE WORLD

THE DIFFERENT FEAR CATEGORIES

The table below identifies **(i)** Our most fundamental fear types, **(ii)** Their root cause and **(iii)** Indicates the ego's proposed solution to mitigate each. The ego aims to ignore the primary underlying cause of our fears and offers solutions that will not work. Since we do not administer the cure directly at the source, is it a surprise that our fear persists?

Fear Type	Root Cause	Ego Solution
Financial	Our Belief in Scarcity	To ruthlessly plunder from and deceive others.
Sickness	Our Bodily Identity	Magical Beliefs (Prescriptions, Remedies, Vaccines etc.)
Powerlessness	Our Belief in Victimhood	Judgment, Attack and Condemnation
Meaninglessness	Lost Awareness of Truth	To substitute with various Idols and Temptations, (Including Specialness)
Isolation and Abandonment	Separation	Special Relationships
The Unknown	Loss of Knowledge and Severance from our True Identity	To increase Fear while becoming more Defensive and Closed-Minded.
Death	Lost Awareness of Truth	Denial, Distraction and Pleasure Seeking

OUR DIFFERENT FEAR TYPES AND THE EGO'S PROPOSE SOLUTION TO MITIGATE EACH

THE INHERITANCE OF FEAR

Fear arises not in a vacuum. It is always the consequence of unloving decisions. These trigger a grim chain of events and induce a foggy state of mind, in which more cursed decisions become probable. As our world becomes clouded, and we begin to settle for any tiny gifts, we can pilfer in the shadowy world of perception. Due to the power of conditioning, the meaningless soon rises to life and becomes very attractive. At this point, we have lost all sight of our former Identity and protect our fragile minds through the dynamics of denial, projection, and dissociation.

We carve various idols out of the dark and begin to interpret them, as our only means of salvation. Our universe becomes one of objects, which all seem separate and unrelated. It is only natural that we conceive things will run out and we will be left deprived. Hence our minds become infiltrated with a fearful belief in Scarcity. There seems to be no end to our torment, and we must find some satisfaction somewhere in this mess. Something to replace the Love and security, we feel denied. So like insects, who swiftly perish when instinctually driven, we likewise feel drawn to the false light of specialness. We begin to crave all empty offerings to fill the void in our souls; something to compensate for our lost knowledge, peace, and bliss. We scavenge the world for all with whom we can forge special relationships. These become our havens of safety in a vola- tile and capricious world and the context, where we hope to find real Love, at last.

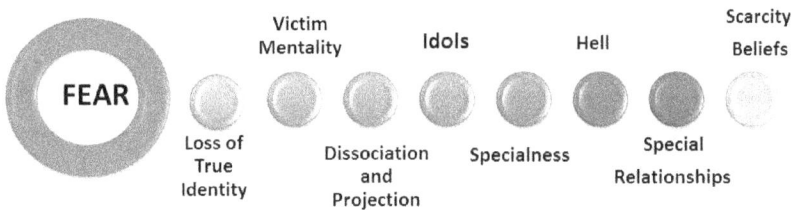

Ultimately, it is our belief in separation which leads to fear, just as surely as the recognition of unity leads to peace. Taking separation to be true, we maliciously judge and condemn, as a strategy for our protection. These measures increase fear and serve as the underlying basis for all inappropriate attacks. Believing in the efficacy of attack, we fully expect it to be reciprocated. Before long, all progress becomes deadlocked due to the unholy alliance of hate, attack, and fear. Since only the fearful can hate; we experience its illusory manifestations from many different vantage points. Likewise, anxiety, sickness, mental instability, psychosis, identity confusion, joylessness, and victimhood all have their roots in fear. Fear precipitates all communication failures because it functions to isolate and alienate.

The fearful are deeply attracted to notions of guilt and sin. They leverage these crazy ego notions to justify erecting a vast network of unneeded barriers and psychological defenses. All fear is powered by our thoughts and wrongful interpretations. From our misplaced ideations, the shadow world gains all its seeming life. The presence of fear is a byproduct of our lost spiritual intimacy and loving connection. Fear like the mythical Hydra may have many heads, but despite its numerous materializations, all its forms encapsulate a single content.

FEAR AND THE EGO

As a divine being, the ego cannot twist your arm, nor control your decision making unless you empower it to do so. It is you that lends it your will. Whenever you are fearful, realize you have invested your chips with the ego. Without all those fearful beliefs, it continually instills and propagates, fear would be impossible. Unfortunately, we have allowed unfounded ego beliefs to become rooted in our hearts and minds. These cover our world under a dark cloud. As a consequence, we have grown increasingly sullen, embittered, and toxic in our attitudes and feel hounded by an ongoing invasion of disturbing thoughts. No longer possessing any clarity or focus, we have become mistrustful of everyone and all newly emerging situations. We have devolved into severely contracted beings and our meager troll-like existence, our hearts find repulsive.

Assuredly, we all have those days when we feel ourselves, as insignificant minions, suffocating in the field of life. Days when we are unsure where to put our next step. Times when we sense invisible forces surrounding us, which we feel powerless to subdue or restrain. Yes, the mind has many insidious snakes. Some we are consciously aware of and others not. It is these hidden and masked snakes that darken the entire landscape of our perception. We must become willing to descend into the viper pit and utilize the flame of our discriminating wisdom to purge all such vermin from our minds.

Fear does not lend itself to direct frontal assault. Any direct attack emphasizes and reinforces the wild notion; it has a reality. The right means to eradicating it is by recognizing that all shadows it casts are chimerical and imaginary and they can only arise in the absence of light. Fear only creeps in when the light has been turned off. No one in their right mind would attack ephemeral shadows born from within. Poisonous weeds can only flourish in the barren soil of our ignorance. Even so, the pseudo-reality of fear becomes strengthened through any analysis and investigation into its essence. The only solution is to switch back on the light. This strategy entails our mental migration to a more loving disposition.

FEAR AS A BYPRODUCT OF EGO DISTORTION

Our complete liberation from fear lies in correcting all erroneous beliefs, we sincerely cherish. This enterprise involves reprogramming the entire foundational template of our thought, at a fundamental level. Implementing surface strategies or mere changes in behavior will not work. Mistaken beliefs have incredible power, for they are the source of all fear and distortion. To be successful in this mission, we must capitalize on our capacities for reason and introspection, to reach new ground. That sacred Terra firma which the ego does not own or lease. On this journey, the recognition dawns that love and fear are polar opposites. They can never be married or meaningfully interfused in any higher relationship.

There is no fear in love, nor love in fear. Nonetheless, we are continuously choosing between these two extremes.

Whenever we yield to weakness and to various temptations, dream idols and false notions of our specialness and superiority, our ability to execute clear-minded intelligent decisions is compromised. Consequently, our will is soon rendered impotent and unable to release us from the corrupt persuasions of the ego.

Whenever we see the dream as our place of salvation, we lose the impartiality needed to recognize Truth. Our self-deceptions are immensely costly since they enable fear to flourish. Honesty, trust, faith, and open-mindedness, in contrast, permit the light already in our minds to shine through it, unimpeded. They reinstate our omnipotence over appearances, and they reveal the Real world. All easier said than done; you may reflect! After all, fearful ego beliefs have become deeply threaded and are now part of our conditioned visceral response. Such tenaciously held beliefs can only be undone by sincerely questioning them and penetrating to their core. In this exposure, their entire lack of validity becomes readily affirmed. Even so, our progress will be thwarted, if we insist on taking the ego as our guide.

The ego's solution is to apply superficial Band-Aids, which are only capable of providing temporary alleviation from pain. It distracts from the real roots of our fear and proposes inefficacious behavioral solutions, guaranteed not to work. It comprehends instinctively that only a fearful mind will ever listen to its insane advice. One of its principal aims, therefore, is to cleverly conceal the full extent of our fears from our direct awareness. It realizes that if we become overwhelmed by fear and trepidation, we will panic and abandon it. Behavioral solutions aspire to teach and reinforce the ill-placed notion that fear is produced by the external world. By denying its real source within, we remain fractured and unable to heal. The outcome of this strategy is all-pervasive in the world. Everywhere we encounter the denial of self-generated fears and behavioral approaches aimed to mitigate their pain. We all avoid facing our core issues and fears head-on.

A drug addict, for example, may attempt alleviation of their essential fears by remaining in a perpetually comatose state. However, every Ostrich has to pull its head out of the sand eventually. Until then, its fear-prone condition only worsens. Others try to conceal their inner emptiness through gambling, hoarding, various shopping addictions, work or pleasure-seeking pursuits. All fail and deprived of their sedative of choice, they cannot even tolerate their own company.

THE WOUNDED VETERAN

Paul was a Vietnam Veteran. There was nothing; he would not do for this Country. The fire of his patriotic pride and passion was always aflame. In '68, at the age of just seventeen, he was restless and enthusiastic to go. Eager to enter those killing fields where he hoped he could die for his Country. His family had always held a proud military tradition. His father and three uncles had experienced the heart of the action in WWII in Russia, Italy, and the Ardennes. His Dad and one brother alone returned from that war. Edward and Albert were both killed. Edward was lost at sea and served on the USS Leopold. Albert died during the Murmansk run and was later buried in Arlington cemetery. As the Battle of the Bulge fizzled out, his father one day rounded up over two dozen German soldiers, without any weapon. They were wonderfully complicit because they were even more terrified of surrendering to the Russkies.

During Vietnam, Paul was sent on many covert operations. As a sniper, he was a Master in stealth and would not even wear his dog tags, to avoid making noise. He excelled in his assignment since they brainwashed him into believing he was taking out a ferocious Communist enemy. From one day to the next, he would remain naively unaware of where he was being deployed, and of who his enemy was. They were just faces popping up from the rice paddies and did not look particularly dangerous, menacing or even armed. When he came back from the war, he started becoming overtly self-destructive and drank heavily. He would typically consume 1.75 liters of vodka a day. He began to suffer from depression and often would alleviate the pain by cutting himself. Many times he was taken away in an ambulance and sometimes just barely survived due to the extent of blood loss. He disliked blacks, but on one occasion he needed a transfusion and was given four pints of blood. After that, his attitude towards blacks changed immensely since he realized the blood which saved his life was donated by an unknown black man or woman.

Many times he was locked away in a psych ward and medicated intensely. He met a team of psychiatrists and was bombarded all the way to neuroleptic Heaven, and still, nothing changed. Something deep within him remained profoundly troubled. He could not allow himself to admit, that those whom he had taken out in the rice fields in Vietnam were merely farmers and peasants. They had nothing at all to do with the vile engines of war and were just trying to make a living in the hot sun. All mothers and fathers, uncles and daughters. He had been leveraged on his patriotism and sold a sweet tasting lie. Over time, the guilt for what he had executed became lodged into the unfathomable reaches of his unconscious because he never could admit his Country had used him so. What the fuck had he done? How could he have allowed himself to be so duped? Such were the questions that bubbled incessantly below in the firmament of his subconscious.

Since he received no answers which brought him Peace, he took the vengeance, his guilt demanded, out on himself. So he made himself into a sacrificial lamb, as a cursory token to alleviate some of God's Wrath. His fear of God was the dominant source of his pain because he could not avoid projecting humanity's maliciousness and evil intent to his Loving Creator. It wasn't until he fully understood that his Creator desired no vengeance or sacrifice that he could finally heal. Eventually, he realized his Creator, being unconditional Love only created the eternally innocent and sinless.

THE CIRCLE OF FEAR

We must reach beyond the ego to undo all fear, it continuously propagates. Unless we voyage courageously into those subaqueous reaches of the mind, we will never bypass the stark foundations from which this ego world arose. Until then, the vision of spirit will remain obfuscated by our fears, and we will not behold the radiant, bliss-filled realm which lies far beyond the body's scope. The body's eyes can only ever witness a world of fear because this cavern of sand and water is itself is a by-product of fear's underpinnings in mind. It was designed specifically with the intention of keeping the "separated" existence alive and well. It serves as both a source and consequence of fear and functions as a shield against the light. This Relative World, it perceives, retains no real existence. It will always remain a place of despair and a thin veil constructed purely from illusions.

Our ignorance, alone, causes the Relative World to appear in our perceptions. The closer we come to Knowledge, the more, this unstable halfway house of insanity and strife vaporizes into non-existence. The body's eyes can only ever perceive the dense, limited and artificial because it was made from the unholy wish to be apart. It can see nothing that makes sense because it stands as an intermediary to the brain, which is incapable of thought. Nonetheless, beneath these dark fear clouds, lies the glorious, resplendent light of our True Being. Fear is powerless to extend past the nebulous haze, to find the Love, in which we were Created. It is like a dirty pair of wellingtons which sully and pollute the clear water, wherever they stomp. In our eternal Home, all worlds disappear in a vast vaporous ocean of formlessness. It is a sacred undifferentiated realm in which no boundaries and separations are possible. The body will be seen to disappear once your consciousness becomes pervaded by light. For this, evolution is demanded in your approach. A simple willingness to let the unworthy go!

> **"The circle of fear lies just below the level the body sees, and seems to be the whole foundation on which the world is based. Here are all the illusions, all the twisted thoughts, all the insane attacks, the fury, the vengeance and betrayal that were made to keep the guilt in place, so that the world could rise from it and keep it**

hidden. Its shadow rises to the surface, enough to hold its most external manifestations in darkness, and to bring despair and loneliness to it and keep it joyless. Yet its intensity is veiled by its heavy coverings, and kept apart from what was made to keep it hidden. The body cannot see this, for the body arose from this for its protection, which depends on keeping it not seen. The body's eyes will never look on it. Yet they will see what it dictates."

[ACIM, T-18.IX.4:1-7]

Fear, then fashioned the entire world we see. All forms, manifestations, contrasts, and shadows, in this endless soup of chiaroscuro, are produced by it. The body, being neutral did not synthesize itself. Its only power is to reflexively respond to all idle purposes the mind invests in it. It is incapable of thought! Instead, like any mindless peon, it functions merely as a servile vessel to convert ideas and notions into actions. It is powerless to attack unless the mind conceives, it is utilized that way.

The body's eyes can never know how this world was made. The physical is incapable of illumination and unable to peer beyond the fear that gave rise to it. It was designed to focus on form and to keep awareness of unity, omnipotence, and formlessness completely out of mind. The ego lives and feasts through the body's eyes and your continued lack of vision guarantees, its endless games of showmanship and deception can go on, indefinitely.

MAN'S MATRYOSHKA DOLL

Fear gives birth to many dark mantles which occlude the natural light of Spirit. In Vedantic literature, these sheaths are known as Koshas and can be considered an array of bodies interposed between our physical appearance and our spiritual reality. They function as dark coverings which keep us ensnared in the web of ignorance. They thus operate to impede vision.

In Vedantic vernacular, Spirit, with its infinite knowledge and potencies, is referred to by such glowing terms as *Atman, Ishvara, Brahman* and *Universal Self.* Spirit's home is the causal body, and this is our highest essence. Its scope transcends the limited capacities of our physical, emotional and intellectual bodies.

The Annamayakosha

The outermost sheath of humanity's Matryoshka doll, *the Annamayakosha*, is the physical body we perceive. This body has no intrinsic intelligence and can only respond reactively and instinctively to the beliefs we project to it. So if we desire to be sick, for any reason, sickness will soon materialize here. Whenever we feel spiritually weary or drained, this body willingly reciprocates by inducing a chronic state of fatigue. This body is nothing more than a dense, conditioned aggregate of the thoughts of our lower mind. It is also known as *food body* since it seems to depend on nutrition to survive. As the least subtle of our bodies, it is furthermost divorced from Spirit.

The Pranamayakosha

This Kosha resides just behind the physical one and is known, also as the *energetic* or *vital body.* Even though it cannot be perceived, it can most certainly be felt. Whenever you are eating wholesome foods, doing intense yogic practices and Sadhana, and avoiding stress, anxiety, fear and negativity, this body feels very energized and well.

Once you liberate this body from toxic energy patterns, you will notice a great increase in your appetite, sexual energy, and overall vitality. Your sleep quality will be most excellent, and you will discover a tremendous new zest for life. This body offers an important layer of protection, and it can buffer you from sickness and *malaise.* There is no point taking any flu shot or vaccination, so long as this body's protection remains secured. However, if you allow this body to become darkened or blocked, you will immediately feel drained, incapacitated and unable to think clearly. This blockage will trigger a loss of appetite and motivation and activate a profound lethargic inertia to pervade your entire being.

The Manomayakosha

The Manomayakosha is connected very fluidly and seamlessly with all our emotions, thoughts and ideations. Whenever you allow feelings of bitterness, unwarranted grief, rejection, and isolation in, this Kosha becomes very dark indeed. If you are feeling unloved, lacking in purposeful direction or riddled with anxiety and uncertainty this body will become very dense and occluded. Other manifestations of interfering agents include erratic behaviors, withdrawal, doubt, mistrust, and confusion. In consequence, you will be increasingly grievance orientated, cynical and frosty to new encounters.

This body acts as the critical intermediary between your spiritual Identity and the mundane conceptions of your lower mind. In particular, those primeval thoughts which are highly reactionary and aggressive or else ones associated with base survival, pleasure-seeking, or unbounded accumulation at the expense of others. Whenever this body is not functioning properly and fails to provide access to the light of your spiritual Self, you can quickly become consumed with negativity and tenaciously adverse to all progress, risk, change and new ideas.

Once this body is unblocked, you will instantly feel centered, equanimous and more open to life. Your disposition will be calm, peaceful and serene and you will exude a quiet confidence that attracts others and inspire trust. Having subdued fear, you will automatically be more adventurous and compassionate and ready to welcome new experiences. You will interpret these encounters as pivotal learning opportunities leading to your spiritual transformation and growth.

The Vijnyanamayakosha

The Vijnyanamayakosha is the wisdom body. Whenever it is healthy, you will find yourself imbued with a very discriminating intellect, incisive reasoning capabilities, and a very heightened intuition. The Holy Spirit works predominantly through this Kosha to reinterpret and correct all erroneous ego beliefs and myths. Once it is opened and communicating, you become healed of your dissociated state and released into the light.

Its highest layers correlate with the development of abstract thinking capabilities and associative reasoning powers. When it is functioning smoothly, you will be able to rapidly penetrate and expose the very foundation of whole beliefs systems, in a flash. See from a far more superior and mature perspective which readily unveils the true content lurking at their core. Contradictions and existential paradoxes are powerless to withstand the light shining through this body. It can thus operate expeditiously to accelerate an evolution in the quality of your thought. Entire glaciers of fear, residing in the lower echelons of your mind can be speedily released, never to burden you again.

Unblocking this Kosha, you become wise, clear-headed, radiant and capable of looking beyond appearances directly into Reality. It teleports you swiftly into new and yet ancient vistas of understanding so that you glimpse the essential essence of all and the authentic face of naked existence.

The Anandamayakosha

The **Anandamayakosha** is the bliss body. It is the Kosha linked with Light, Truth, Peace, and Enlightenment. Here all is resolved, and you become restored to the unity and Knowledge of the One-Mind. Since you now perceive through the perfection of Whole-Mind; you experience the Buddha-verse of Nirvana directly. All is spontaneously re-vealed in its true splendor, and seen through the undefiled light of Spirit. Here time and form are entertained no more, for you have entered the realm of the Eternal. Fear be-comes impossible because all hindrances of the lower four bodies have been transcended. The fearful are merely those who feel powerless because they lack Knowledge and certainty. Their abiding state of ignorance (**Avidya**) accumulates and cross-associates over time, placing them in a living hell. Each of the lower four bodies arises from your identification with false and limiting constructs. Be-liefs that nevertheless can be easily displaced and undone. As a composite, they form into the **circle of fear** which surrounds our mind and obfuscates our spiritual reality. Fear is the invisible content, from which all internal bodies are fabricated, apart from the causal body of light, known in Buddhism as the **Dharmakāya**. It is fear alone which makes them all seem substantial.

FEAR, A SPINNER OF THE ILLUSORY

"My thoughts are images that I have made."

[ACIM, Workbook Lesson 15]

Some have experienced a spiritual, mystical or near death experience (**NDE**) which hammered home the enduring realization: *This world is spun entirely from within*. The natural illumination of Enlightenment likewise produces direct experiential evidence of this mystical insight. Once awakened, we become strikingly aware, that the entire perceived universe is just a blank receptacle of our ideations. The fearful world, we picture is just a by-product of our fearful beliefs, projected outward. All the same, since our thoughts first become transmuted and transmogrified into images before being projected, we do not readily recognize this world, as our projection. Nevertheless, such forms perfectly reflect the underlying content of our beliefs. Images have no power since they are merely passive reflections. They derive all their persuasive power through your belief in them. All fearful images will be erased from your perception once you have corrected all mistaken beliefs. Unless you choose to do so, the underlying fears will remain, and become a breathing ground for further illusions and unhappiness.

Pure love sees nothing at the level of form; it is wholly formless. Fear, nonetheless, has a tremendous investment in form and cannot exist apart from it. The ego has always been the joker in the pack, and it maintains the mirage of its existence by keeping fear alive and well nourished. It releases a Pandora box of illusions upon which your eyes then feast. Through presenting various terrifying forms and sensual attractions, it hopes to tempt you into its snares. Its goal is to keep you identified with the dream of fear. Your failure to meaningfully interrogate and relinquish all mistaken beliefs is what fuels all illusions.

Many are fooled by the perceived universe while believing the unperceived and hidden remain powerless. This position is pure nonsense since unconscious beliefs carry tremendous power and resilience. They proceed to shape all your emotions, motivations, and perceptions and their insidious influence can erode your self-esteem, destroy your confidence and contaminate your willpower. Fundamentally they operate to interpose a screen of illusion before your natural awareness. Intractable ego beliefs influence all that appears to happen. Nothing exists outside you, nor apart from your mind. Not recognizing this, is self-deception and it stands as the only barrier between you and Truth.

Once ego beliefs become unconscious, they gain deep roots and slowly poison your mind system. The projection of which is the fear-filled world you see. Thus, you now witness so many Self-obscuring reflections in the mirror of perception. Consequently, fear acquires a very sound basis for continued belief and a strong foothold in your thought. Identifying with the external manifestations of fear, you fail to spot their Source within. However, there alone is the Holy Sanctuary where all terrifying images can be readily released.

"Fear has made everything you think you see. All separation, all distinctions, and the multitude of differences you believe make up the world. They are not there. Love's enemy has made them up. Yet love can have no enemy, and so they have no cause, no being and no consequence. They can be valued, but remain unreal.

They can be sought, but they can not be found. "

[ACIM, WB.130.4:1-7]

Perhaps you think the body exists independently from your mind. In truth, fear produced the body and endowed it with the capacity to see and hear the world of form. Your progress accelerates once you embrace this flawless wisdom. The ego's central purpose for the body is as a vehicle of separation. It wants to drive it into the ground to promote its endless dreams of specialness. Likewise, it treats it contemptuously; more like a rag to satiate all its desires and for launching vicious attacks. All of which causes you to fall prey to a multitude of temptations. It is inevitable that harboring such an uninspiring, second-rate conception of your Home will produce disheartening beliefs and thoughts of vulnerability.

Even so, the body's senses are senses without sense. None can see, nor hear but only represent to their maker, that which he chooses to witness. Thought and form are not two, but one! All appearances and forms are products of the lower mind and the inevitable consequence of miscreating with the ego. This lower mind is the repository of all unreal thoughts and is, therefore, the comfortable down-stairs crash-pad where the ego likes to hang out. In summary, the body is a projection of the lower mind, and it implements a dense covering over reality. It is entirely mindless since it can share no connection with spirit. Nonetheless, being the ego's home and ally, it is conferred with all forms of exotic intelligence. Yes, the ego likes to invest nothingness with value and seeks to raise each flimsy and meretricious attraction into an idol, that it can deploy to screen the real.

Identification with the body leads to fear, and it opens the floodgates for all forms of magical belief to enter. The world of separation reinforces beliefs that aspects of Mind can be genuinely separate. It is all a cunning game of legerdemain because without a body, you would never believe or affirm such a world. Ask, what is Cause and what is Effect? Are we merely looking then at a deceiving screen of effects? One in which the body and its senses serve as a replacement for vision and then proceed to substantiate all ego beliefs in sin. Sin is sacred to the ego, and it pivots around this totem pole to support all its wet dreams of self-preservation and one-upmanship.

So you meander about, comparing yourself with other bodies, rags-to-rags, and dust-to-dust. Some may glow a little more brightly for a while, but it is not long before they too become lackluster and broken-winged. In some, the lights go out all too soon. There are no candles seen in the windows anymore. Others are oxygen starved and are hollowed out and desiccated even before they descend from the red carpet. A brief sojourn on psycho-planet is all they have before the roller coaster swoons into the void of the dispirited.

The profusion of cranial indentations, exsanguinated visages, and sagging flesh cogently reflect the impure thoughts of their thinker. Dried up and robbed of all vitality, they finally come to welcome death. Even crying out for it in a feverish pitch while wailing all the way to the graveyard. Sickness and suffering are their gods, and their dilapidated bodies serve as a testament to their guilt. Fearing God's vengeance, they initiate preemptive strikes against themselves. Thus, their bodies become chiseled and gashed with scars and painted with stripes which proudly depict His villainous and vengeful intent for all to see. Hence, does God seem unjust and merciless and impotent to rescue His Creation.

As soon as the ego is ready to call it a day, it gladly summons death to provide a reprieve from fearful dreams. Speedily death arrives exactly as invited. Sometimes, with a great show of flash and dash and at other times with a whimper. Even so, being an illusion itself, it can never amount to anything more than an exclamation point between sentences. Soon another dream rushes in to paint a happier face on the dummy of our fictional hero. Yes, the show must go on, so long as the essential presence of fear which rules all dreams remains unresolved.

The container is not the content, and the wrapping is not the gift. Do not be fooled by the picture but look only to the veracity of its underlying content. No container can be fearful if its content be not true. You can never separate the dream from the dreamer's mind, but you can certainly choose to wake up. You accomplish this by rigorously questioning the fallacious foundation upon which all fear-based dreams rest. Fear remains forever powerless to show anything that is real. All mistaken beliefs are rapidly smoked and consumed in the bonfire of Knowledge, and the certitude of Spirit.

THE CONSPIRACY OF TIME

Whenever we are truly present, we can experience no fear. Fear only arises out of all our defenses, projections and foolish fantasies. For we retain the firm belief that time has the power to dispossess us of something truly valuable. We become immensely fearful whenever we cerebrate losing the treasures, we cherish. Such chosen pearls may be of our health, privilege or some special dream of wealth and power. Fear is always a consequence of our partiality and attachment. While we continue to esteem the illusions of the Relative World, fear will remain.

Fear uses Time ingeniously in a cunning attempt to demonstrate its reality. Time, like form, is just another face fear masquerades under to add credibility to its deception. Temporal ambiguity and indecision are akin to the mascara, fear puts on, to hide its true content from the light. Not seeing things wholly and purely in the naked present, we endlessly shadow box in the dark. By skillfully misdirecting our energies and distracting us, it extinguishes all hopes of overcoming it.

Time has no power to take anything that is Real; it can only ever dispossess us of illusions. Only the worthless can be flushed away in the sinkhole of time while the treasure of the infinite is always available now. Time and form have no meaning apart. They represent two aspects of a singular framework of illusions. Time convinces you the show of form is in progress while form itself is the show. Their unified deception can be quite mesmerizing. Fear being the time-bound emotion cannot exist or be experienced, whenever time is absent. Without time there can be no fear, and without fear, there can be no time. Fear, therefore, emphasizes the continuity of past and future and it glosses rapidly over the present.

In fear's blind eyes, the cause of the future is the past, while the present is entirely non-existent. The immediate is interpreted as nothing more than a halfway house between the past and future where only hopeless vagabonds, hippies, tramps, and drunks bother to hang out. Maybe there is room too for the odd mystic or quack. Few realize that here is the golden Gateway to Eternity. The yellow brick road to a nowhere paradise, on which, fear becomes finally exposed.

So long as you sip from its concoction of delusion, fear lingers and sniggers in the dark because it knows it can continue to establish its empires in the realm of temporal causality. Nonetheless, Truth bows not to fear, and heeds not, fear's silly notions on causality. It does not enter the illusory to prove itself real nor does it pander to the loud, obnoxious voices of the dead. It knows that once paraded into the light, the nonexistent will quickly disappear like dewdrops before the sun. Time and fear are completely powerless before Truth. Neither can hold a candle to the magnificence and grandeur, silently revealed in the present moment. The present is the unassailable treasury of the forever Real. The future has no existence! Its many-faced deception is driven entirely by your impure desires, unholy intentions and ego needs for vengeance.

Any moment, you can drop all skeletons and fearful beliefs and decide to carry them no longer. Nonetheless, it is only NOW, that such beliefs can be relinquished. NOW is the moment to unburden yourself. This instant extends the sole portal into the vertical dimension of the timeless. Follow any other direction, and you will become lost. For you are choosing to allow illusions, be your guide; and so choosing to fashion your future into a mirror replica of your past.

You will willingly rid yourself of all skeletons once you know how much they cost! For you are continuously being humiliated, scorned and belittled in the minefield of life. Molded and shaped into some ridiculous image, seen in clay, while your radiant Reality perpetually eludes you. Self-purification leads to hallowed ground and the Kingdom of Immortals. All the same, fear craftily utilizes the past as its feeding grounds. From this disenchanted wasteland, it vomits out all inner toxins and bile into an imaginary and uncertain future. Even so, all fear is disbanded in the light of your Holy Vision. Vision penetrates beyond, and releases all self-made deceptions!

"Fear is not of the present, but only of the past and future, which do not exist. There is no fear in the present when each instant stands clear and separated from the past, without its shadow reaching out into the future. Each instant is a clean, untarnished birth, in which the Son of God emerges from the past into the present. And the present extends forever. It is so beautiful and so clean and free of

guilt that nothing but happiness is there. No darkness is remembered, and immortality and joy are now."

[ACIM, T-15.I.8:2-7]

FEAR IS VAPORIZED IN THE TRUE PRESENT

This instant, seen truly, holds the inexhaustible treasury, you have always sought. In its luminous light frame, lies our imperishable Home, Perfect Knowledge and awareness of everlasting Grandeur. Eternity is no mental abstraction but an ever-abiding Reality *Here-Now,* for the taking. Sadly, its splendor and magnificence go unnoticed because of our unholy alliance with the ego. Nonetheless, once we erase all misconceptions, our understanding runs limpid, and all our thoughts become Creative and Miraculous, in nature. Then we are immediately transported into the unconditioned space of the Enlightened! Spontaneously shedding the soiled impure garments of time for the unfading raiment of the immaculate and indestructible. Our new attire is non-corporeal because it evidences our original perfection. It witnesses very persuasively the pestilential forces of fear; we have finally vanquished. Now as we diffuse the eternal perfume indiscriminately in all directions, we effortlessly shower gifts of miracles and healing to all.

Yes, it had rained streams of misery, tears, and blood for endless eons, and you shape-shifted into some pathetic creature that groveled in the dark. Existing as a mindless surrogate and troll that callously mocked all your former glory. But now you drink from the chalice of never-ending bliss and have become one of the immortals. So you take your rest in the paradisiacal void of the truly Creative, Potent and Meaningful and recognize all as flawless in its beauty and serenely beatific in its essence.

Ascending back to your original face, you are in for a shock. For you recognize most compellingly, the full extent of your former presbyopic condition. You become aghast by the degree fear reigned unimpeded while you slept wretchedly in the Siberian Gulags of the phenomenal and relative. That drug of your Self-forgetfulness induced a tenebrous haze over your mind, in which so many insipid skeletons sprang to life. Various idols and fantasies rose to prominence, which shrouded you further under the dark veil of ignorance. You had roamed about in a bleak land-scape with the carnivorous dogs of misery and despair as your only bedfellows. Gratefully, the quiet revelatory power of the present came to your rescue. Thus were you liberated from the pernicious influence of all wrong-minded beliefs, born in time and came to witness a luminous, happy and vibrant world emerge from the ashes; One that foreshadowed and presaged your inevitable awakening.

It is inevitable that a mind blinded by past torments and vengeful acts will seek retribution. In its tortured state, it remains conflicted and no longer available to current events. Obsessed with the past, it seeks every opportunity to recreate and avenge it in the present. So does its future become predetermined, and salvation a mere game of exacting vengeance! Thus at the midnight hour, it roams the neighborhood looking to gorge itself on some new prize; and to exsanguinate another victim.

George Santayana once declared: *"Those who don't remember the past are condemned to live by it."* In truth, it is: *"Those who <u>do</u> remember the past who are doomed to live by it.* For all who cling to old beliefs and dead patterns precondition their mindsets to filter out the real. They shut out the light which could wholly heal them. Most often, our thoughts lack the thrust and escape velocity needed to surmount the gravitational fields of our insanity. In the resulting implosion, we become circumvented and fall back into the black hole of our humdrum existence. Then sell all our stock in the present to purchase the illusion of time.

There is nothing wrong with the past. Depending on how it was engaged, it may have been a boon or a curse. All our memories, inspiration and former passions are traced back to it like a jet stream. Nonetheless, all transformation, it has brought is either meaningful now, or it was entirely illusory and without effect. If we have genuinely understood its lessons, then we have hit the jackpot. If no progressive changes have flowered and our thinking patterns remain closed and unshaken, then it has been time wastefully squandered, chasing chimerical shadows in an empty hall of mirrors. We are then doomed to repeat the same mistakes over-and-over.

To enter the gates of Truth, we must become capable of interpreting all through the impartial eyes of wisdom. The useful and expedient should be retained and the ineffectual quickly discarded. He, who devotes himself to the worthless gets caught in the thick and thorny briars of illusion. Apotheosizing phantoms of the mind, he takes a sure path deeper into hell. There he remains condemned, to suffer pain needlessly and until, that instant when he shifts his devotion. The hole you are in is a consequence of your adoration and faithfulness to the ego. Upholding all its nonsense opinions, futile strategies and unfair judgments is equivalent to holding a sword against yourself. Caving to its meretricious enticements and fleeting pleasures weakens your will and denudes you of clarity. A part of you knows what has not worked, will never work. The willingness to freely let it all go is, therefore, is but a sign of restored sanity. From this seed will sprout a progressive and open future. One vibrant and joyful and incomparable to your past. Very soon, your healed state of mind will be in evidence to all.

ESCAPING THE DREAM

Every moment, we choose between freedom and slavery. We continue to work jobs we hate, attend events we abhor and stay in toxic relationships. Fear has poisoned our minds and crippled our every move. Embracing freedom seems too much of a burden. It seems far easier to remain distracted and to simply let the superficial, surface activities of everyday life rule the show. When we obviate the power of our free will, we do not recognize the damage this inflicts. It is the decision to endure suffering instead of bliss, and it enables apparitions to rule us.

The dream of fear is caused by ourselves. Only by embracing our reality as its dreamer, can we transcend its bleak context! Healing and release can occur only at the level of cause. Until we administer the cure at this level, our suffering and bondage will remain and just transmogrify into new ingenious forms. It is impossible to awaken unless you become willing to stop identifying with the dream of the Relative World. This is known as the path of Self-remembrance. The Ancient Siddha, Patanjali describes the crucial step needed with the simple maxim: "**Chitta Vritti Nirodhah**." It translates into; "*Cease all identification with* *the fluctuations of consciousness."* What are these fluctuations in consciousness, you may ask? Firstly they engender all our thoughts, emotions, judgments and insights. Additionally, they include all our conceptual understandings, aspirations, inspirations, passions and biases. In fact, they embrace the totality of what we know as life. Only a mind relinquished of all unreal thoughts is free. Only such an awareness enters the pure non-differentiated space.

No thought has power unless you entrust it with such potential. This crucial insight leads to Self-mastery. All your ideations become imaged as phantom appearances that remain powerless to guide to reality. They may tempt and attract, at times, and thus they keep you hypnotized and spellbound to the dream. But you can see through all their empty offerings and cheap seductions if you wish. For you are the pure undifferentiated awareness, from which they all arise. Your mind is a highly potent, fathomless and deathless awareness from which all worlds emerge and again disappear. Your true Identity is as the limitless sky behind the scenes. One forever tacit and intangible since it cannot be sensorily or phenomenally detected. Practicing this technique, you become centered, calm and equanimous. You were foolishly identifying with the clouds and ignored your real treasure-house. So you tossed mindlessly in your sleep, in a severely drugged and terrorized state. Once your consciousness became seduced into beggary of the objective realm, you became diminished into a troll-like image in your mind-generated dream. Beguiled into a hearty identification with your projections erased your chances of transcending the objective-subjective duality.

The world is not the problem! The mind which continuously identifies with it is the source of all misery! Dreamers do not know they dream. Otherwise, they would readily awaken. Investing all their attention and time entertaining images and phenomenal appearances entices them to forget unequivocally who is the projectionist. So they live out their lives in the turbulent sea of the phenomenal world. All the same, identifying exclusively with one-half of a duality cannot lead to Self-realization. One must embrace existence in its totality and from both the inside and outside at once. In a flash of insight, one unerringly recognizes that the subjective produces the objective and this is the critical ingredient needed for transcendence.

The ego is that *Deus ex Machina* responsible for perpetrating all fear-based psychodramas! It exists as an imaginary totem pole around which are chained all your fearful beliefs. While you identify with fear, this totem pole seems immensely concrete and incontestable. Thus you pay homage to the various ideologies and belief systems that construct your fear-based world. You fail to peer behind the curtain. If you did, you would know that there is nothing there. All you have experienced has been the wild imaginings of a feverish mind and one that dreams of a power greater than God Himself.

The ego is that unreality which continuously weaves more fear-based solutions into your mind. It is incapable of vision, and it has no wisdom to impart. In fact, the ego is the only barrier to the restoration of vision. Empowering a wooden statue of the Buddha will not lead to the Buddha-mind. The undefiled state of consciousness known as Bodhicitta cannot be known through the path of idolatry. Can the fearful images perceived in the mirror of existence inform the projectionist that they are fabricated entirely out of his ignorance? These dark images automatically disappear once genuinely understood as mere hallucinations. Fear can only reside in the mind that has temporarily lost access to Knowledge. Its powerlessness and insubstantiality become evident once you progress beyond its false foundation.

This heavy-seeming barrier, this artificial floor that looks like rock, is like a bank of low dark clouds that seem to be a solid wall before the sun. Its impenetrable appearance is wholly an illusion. It gives way softly to the mountain tops that rise above it, and has no power at all to hold back anyone willing to climb above it and see the sun. It is not strong enough to stop a button's fall, nor hold a feather. Nothing can rest upon it, for it is but an illusion of a foundation. Try but to touch it and it disappears; attempt to grasp it and your hands hold nothing.

[ACIM, T-18.IX.6:1-6]

FEAR IS BORN FROM WITHIN

Our common sense opinions, though abundantly commonplace, are often lacking in sense. For instance, our gut instincts inform us very compellingly that fear is a byproduct of an external world. Hence we come to believe over time that our angst, trepidation, and sense of foreboding are being triggered by events happening out there. However, our visceral instincts are unreliable witnesses. They are powerless to reveal the unreality of what we perceive because they matured from within this hallucinatory manifold. They cannot transmit the wisdom that fear develops first in our thought nor teach that the landscape of perception is a sense generated end-product of our fear. This critical recognition we fail to make. Even so, taking the responsibility that comes with this insight is key to self-empowerment, and release from all pseudo-bondage. It enables us to awaken from our sleep of denial and escape the incredible terror of living under the ego's regime. It transports into the hall of wisdom and allows to vacate the sweat-filled corridors of ignorance!

"There is an instant in which terror seems to grip your mind so wholly that escape appears quite hopeless. When you realize, once and for all, that it is you you fear, the mind perceives itself as split. And this had been concealed while you believed attack could be directed outward, and returned from outside to within. It seemed to be an enemy outside you had to fear. And thus a god outside yourself became your mortal enemy; the source of fear."

[ACIM, WB.196.10:1-5]

Once the profound realization sinks in that fear is internally derived, the mind does not know what to do. You had always shifted the responsibility outward; and badgered and victimized others for your individual faults and weakness. Now you feel pressured to take a voyage inward that will expose all dark cornerstones of your endogenous thought. The moment you have this incredible epiphany, your belief system becomes irreparably shattered. The knowledge that fear has no power in itself; and that all its apparent power arises from your thoughts and interpretations can be revelatory and ground-breaking. It paves the way for the complete relinquishment of ignorance and your restoration to right-mindedness. It is a Holy Instant in which you enter the gateway to light and exit the space-time existence. For a long while, however, your mind will seem split and at war with itself. This conflicted state remains until the production engines of your fear can be shut down. This step involves identifying which your core beliefs are mistaken and therefore, fear producing.

"For once you understand it is impossible that you be hurt except by your own thoughts, the fear of God must disappear. You cannot then belief that fear is caused without. And God, Whom you had thought to banish, can be welcomed back within the holy mind He never left."

[ACIM, WB.196.8:3-5]

THE REAL ROOTS OF FEAR

The ego thrives on fear. Fear is the whip; it masterfully commands to force you to listen to its insane ranting. Once it succeeds in infusing fear, it has won the battle in your mind. The real roots of fear lie in your unconscious guilt. Guilt's treacherous, (albeit covert) presence provides the soil from which the seeds of evil and sin extend their tendrils upwards to become fragrant flowers on the surface. Inhaling these suffocating blossoms produces instant death. They smell so sweet and stupefying that they lull and captivate your senses. In your intoxicated mindless state, you become quick prey for the agents of darkness.

The separated condition is a fearful swamp of carnivorous reptiles from which an exceedingly mephitic odor persistently emanates. This noxious scent gushes upward like a geyser to preach your fear, victimhood, and vulnerability to all. The intense separation you feel is nothing but guilt's projection, and the ego is the separated condition personified. Spirit recognizes only that which is unified and One. Sadly, in the imaginary world of post-separation, Spirit and its Knowledge have become almost entirely blocked from our awareness. It is a futile strategy to dismiss your feelings of fear, while still believing in fear's ultimate reality. This game plan constitutes a form of self-attack through denial, and the ego welcomes it. Attack of any kind, whether directed within or without licenses the ego's methods. Denying our experience of pseudo-separation precludes all healing. The solution is letting the light of genuine forgiveness shine unconditional Love into the Relative World. Boundless love desires only to bless and heal. So are you restored to the vision of spirit and the recognition of innocence! Now with the Holy Grail uncovered, your perception becomes truly luminous. As all beliefs in guilt are annihilated, you drop all interest in attack and sin. You will settle only for the unassailable gifts of the eternal. Rejuvenated and nourished you relinquish that cardboard diet of illusions and false hopes. The springtime of your complete deliverance is now at hand.

The "**Law of Belief**" states that "**You will believe others can do to you, exactly what you believe you can do to them.**" Unconscious guilt is our original sin. Adam could never extricate it from his mind despite his overzealous use of projection. Soon the denied became unconscious. Our mission is to wake up Adam, simply by awakening ourselves. We accomplish this by relinquishing the ego as our shield against the light and by ceasing to sanctify its brutal tactics and unholy methods. Adam chose to become a victim in the dream he made. In his madness, he now roams the relative world where he feels deeply split due to his unwise investments. He demands a foolish fantasy of innocence and specialness, for himself alone. Hence his mind remains fragmented and discombobulated into a gazillion different pieces! In this powerful explosion, fear was born. Judgment is the carving blade by which we keep our "separated" existence alive and well. All this works to reinforce attack, rage, condemnation, and retribution and it calls for a multiplicity of unneeded defenses. The one goal of judgment is to prevent our unconscious guilt from ever being uncovered and healed.

Where once stood Truth, now appears the Gollum of the ego and the ghetto of the Relative World. Yes, line up ladies, and gentleman, hell has finally come to town. Have you not heard, that we have finally succeeded in decimating and dismantling Truth and sawing the Holy Virgin in half. Yes, our insanity knows no bounds. To declare that none of this ever happened seems the height of foolishness and self-deception. Nonetheless, our image is not our reality, only a projection in our dream of separation. It thrives through all idols, attachments, and false identifications we cherish. These constitute the psychological forces that keep us in bondage.

The poisons of attachment and delusion deny us freedom. Our complete impartiality and non-identification alone can awaken us from the dream of fear. In this liberation process, each transforms into a glowing portrait of wholeness, potency, purity and newfound wisdom to become a beacon to all who walk the world in rags, searching for bottles on the beach. Meretricious gifts lead nowhere; esteeming the valueless distorts our thinking, and it renders our will impotent. Our Real Identity emerges in an aureole of radiance, to the extent that we put out the trash.

Until then the tragicomedy of fear must go on. It is a cruel drama in which illusions seem to possess a commensurate power with Truth. One in which a million nightmarish imaginations materialize from the penumbra, to thread their claws into the fabric of our life experience. The bleak enumeration includes various fantasies concerning bodies, suffering, heroic death and destruction, and the jewels of pseudo-love and specialness. In all forms of ego salvation, lifetimes are wasted chasing empty things. In each, you grow bitter and dry, then howl and scream at the injustice of it all. It seems the Treasury of Fantasyland has not made good on your deposit. Finally, you welcome death. To paraphrase, Shakespeare, your life will have been another tale told by a madman full of anger and fury signifying nothing. Your one alternative is to embrace the Holy Spirit's Wisdom as your source of guidance; then skillfully engage your intuition to adventure in an entirely new direction. This is the meaningful voyage that transcends the ego and eradicates all fear. Executing rational and sane decisions blazes a pathway to Perfect Knowledge. Illusions will not withstand the light, you now command, because twisted interests are no longer your game.

> **"God's Son is not a traveller through outer worlds. However holy his perception may become, no world outside himself holds his inheritance."**

[ACIM, T-13.VII.13:5-6]

Listen not to the voices of the dead for answers—embrace only what you have known firsthand. The ego seeks to derail, at every opportunity, and you will find its witnesses posted everywhere. Compelling as they may seem, they are nothing but projections of your lower mind. Do not sign on the dotted line, and see how increasingly frantic and savage, it becomes, in its measures to persuade you. It will audaciously preach from its podium that only emptiness and insanity lie within. An ocean of nothingness in which you will lose all sense of identity and drown; for here lies the void of your self-annihilation. Its real fear is one of being finally unveiled and exposed for what it is. You gain in strength as you renounce its thought and accept the Voice for Truth in its place. A Voice that quietly and humbly reminds that in you, lies the prevailing power in the universe. Nonetheless, this power can be used as a help or hindrance, to serve creation or miscreation. Whenever you miscreate, your fear increases.

The ego personifies all that works against your best interests. It is a non-entity born out of your unwholesome desires for vengeance and temptation. It exerts a domineering and tyrannical influence over your decisions, and yet you continue to license your power to it. Do not divert your eyes from this sly magician's hands. Even though they release a superabundance of mind-numbing effects into your perception—all arise from a single fearful belief. Undo any of its fear's branches and innumerable miscreations are instantaneously released from the dark screen before you. Then the deathless light within will radiate outward to illuminate your perception. It emerges from that part of your mind where fear can never go.

> **"It is not necessary to follow fear through all the circuitous routes by which it burrows underground and hides in darkness, to emerge in forms quite different from what it is. Yet it *is* necessary to examine each one as long as you would retain the principle that governs all of them. When you are willing to regard them, not as separate, but as different manifestations of the same idea, and one you do not want, they go together. The idea is simply this: You believe it is possible to be host to the ego or hostage to God. This is the choice you think you have, and the decision that you believe that you must make."**

[ACIM, T-15.X.5:1-5]

The imprint of our ego thought is imaged in our shifting moods and endless vacillations. It is there in our idols, never-ending preferences, foolhardy ideas and miscreative conceptions. Beneath all this, lies our underlying hopelessness, misery, and despair. The ego charters us on a doomed course, and it offers no grounds for stability and peace. On this path we interpret God, as a loveless dictator since we can never veto His Will. We prefer to remain as deplorable minions, surrogates, and sycophants in Hell, rather than acknowledge our sublime Creatorship and eternal inheritance. Such is its bait. It tempts with the prospect of becoming masters in our private worlds. It does not reveal; that there can be no true Mastery in a kingdom of illusion. All who entertain phantasms become slaves and soon lose all freedom, power, and control. Reacting to our mind-driven hallucinations increases fear. It can never subdue it.

Paying homage to the non-existent is not the golden pathway to emancipation. Amplifying distortions born of fear and faithfully pandering to them can only enslave. Once we deny our fundamental Self, fear steps in to miscreate. Much arises in the mists of our distorted perceptions, and none of it is true. This chamber of horror and idolatry is where sickness, suffering, cruelty, mercilessness, misconception, and unhappiness come to rule the day. We become over-whelmed by a multitude of psychoses, neuroses, suicides, identity splits, and futile passions! There is so much trash littering our path that it can be hard to believe fear made them all up. Fear blinds and makes us strangers to our-selves. This loss of identity erodes our faith and seals our imagined bondage.

> **"Fear must make blind, for this its weapon is: That which you fear to see you cannot see. Love and perception thus go hand in hand, but fear obscures in darkness what is there."**
>
> [ACIM, WB.130.2:4-5]

> **"Fear is a stranger to the ways of love. Identify with fear, and you will be a stranger to yourself."**
>
> [ACIM, WB.160.1:1-2]

THE TRUE COST OF FEAR

Once you glimpse a fraction of fear's true cost, you will hasten to obliterate its insidious influence from your thought. Because it erodes all your life potential and it functions as a fatal poison that infiltrates the well of your vitality. Where it is present, ignorance grows, and confusion and contradictions thrive. Fearing our mind's miscreations, we remain hidden beneath the dark cloak of ignorance. Never questioning its manifestations, the right-minded understandings that could free us, become screened from our awareness. Fear incapacitates our powers for abstraction, induction, inference, and generalization. Fear mongering thoughts induce chronic closed-mindedness and inflexibility which tarnishes our reason.

Anything properly understood cannot be fearful because Reality is not fearful. It is only illusions that promote fear. Nonetheless, fear's miscreations, darken the mind and obscure vision. The fearful mind is a dissociated one, and it lacks the wisdom and transparency of Whole-Mind. Endlessly unleashing its dark judgments, it defeats its best interests and becomes terrified—much, as a child is of the shadows seen on his wall at night. Likewise, we are the ones who invest all shadowy reflections in the world with all their power.

"For fear lies not in reality, but in the minds of children who do not understand reality. It is only their lack of understanding that frightens them, and when they learn to perceive truly they are not afraid."

[ACIM, T-11.VIII.14:4-5]

"Nothing you understand is fearful."

[ACIM, T-14.VI.1:2]

THE SEVERANCE FROM OUR REAL IDENTITY

Is it evident yet the full hand the ego has in crafting all the misery and mischief in the world? And what a masterwork it has formed! An intricate soulless frame, jeweled with a profusion of callous brutalities, mangled bodies, needless suffering and never-ending disasters. One foaming with untamable hate from which rain an unremitting cascade of pointless tears and futile bloodshed. Into this elaborate burdensome frame minds devoid of all sensitivity and compassion come to find themselves! Here in this barren landscape, ice-cold Ötzis and loveless creatures, with self-serving agendas carry out their reigns of mass confusion and terror. What a jaw-dropping Specter it is! Every crack is littered abundantly with bias, misrepresentation, deception and the runny diarrhea of ill-formed thoughts. The overbearing stench of insincerity, fabricated lies, dispassion, conceit and hostile indifference seep up from every fissure in this tangled glacial cesspit that the ego so loves to glorify.

The world is now an artless megalith of convoluted nonsense and we urgently need a spam filter to siphon out all the senseless information bombardment. From every angle it is replete with pretense, hypocrisy, and flimflam posturing and the duplicitous masquerading of free-wheeling Chameleons. The hijacking of our minds is almost complete. We have rapidly morphed into zombies and automatons for the profiteering enterprises and are slaves to the great Borg Mind. The end-product of all our ingenuity and progress is a kind of living death! Yes, death pervades the engine that presently rules the world. Do not let all the sophistication, complexity, and frenzied activity fool you for a moment.

The devil is in the machine, and it is a beast with many heads and countless limbs whose invisible reach extends everywhere. This succubus aims to suck on all our lifeblood and sweat so that it can transmute this into more mechanisms of control and subjugation. Suddenly, I find I am tossed outside myself into a helter-skelter montage of clay and rubble. As my consciousness, regains its bearings and coagulates, I see the real picture. Fear speaking its urgent and dire message through a plethora of forked tongues. It is there in every gesture, expression, and emotion and it pervades the worlds of the microscopic just as effortlessly as the cosmological. Now it seeps downward into our polypeptides, infusing each with its lethal toxins.

To my dismay, I find it is cellularly encoded into the imprint of our mitochondrial DNA, just as extensively as the austere regions of the cosmos. Within a moment, it becomes playful and starts bouncing over and back across the corpus callosum, as if it were having a game of pong. Its work, of reprogramming the template of our thoughts complete, it moves on. Minds implode, and ghostlike figures emerge. Psychologically confident beings who were once boisterous and exuberant rapidly transfigure into pale imitations who lie stooped, lifeless and broken. Fear's fatal energies noble aim is to shape all events and decisions and remodel the universe. Its dark mantle soon extends outwards past Easter Island, Urantia, and the rings of Saturn. Then it proceeds to engrave a blazing trajectory of antimatter across the night sky as it heads onwards to Betelgeuse and the great beyond.

The proliferation of addictions, pharmaceutical abuses, political corruptions, corporate deifications and good old boy cronyism are not an accident. They arise in that mushroom cloud where full-scale severance from our true Identity, has been secured. We are left with no other option except to mope about the planet in a severely disconnected state, as neurotics, psychopaths, sociopaths, hoarders, shopaholics and work-obsessed freaks and to participate in this wild circus of hostile animals. Soon baseless profanities come pissing out our ears showering the world with the searing pain of our divine dejection. The only cure is projecting our relentless inner turmoil and unmitigated angst to this jungle of insanity. Nonetheless, all the vulgar and murderous reflections we see in this mirror merely serve as our patsy in our perpetual disinformation campaign against ourselves. Meanwhile, creeping up from the seedy undergrowth are ever new thorns that bleed. Those of endless prevarication, vacillation, and muddle-minded confusion and there is a muffled whispering of falsehoods from a voice, which dares not know reality, up close and personal. Even so, we graciously sip from this chalice, the vile and poisonous concoction that seals our faith.

We must find meaning at any cost, even if only through exalting the meaningless and infusing it with false hope and life. So we dress up the dummy, pamper it and then apotheosize it into a living god. The only compensation, the ego knows for countering our inner emptiness and despair is through erecting some eminent and grandiose self-image that we will cherish. Thus, each sets out to craft some illustrious and dignified self-concept which he can then proudly present to the world. This elaborate and elegant packaging is nothing but a fly trap to lure suckers into our snares.

A superficial mask of our betrayal, designed to prevent the Sudra class of untouchables from entering our dens. No! There can be no unsolicited intrusions into our inner Sancta-Sanctorum. The real face of the ego must never be exposed because here lies all its secret vaults, hidden treasures and prime mechanisms of deception.

The building blocks for constructing this self-image are many. It encompasses our values, virtues, accomplishments, credentials, experiences, natural and supernatural abilities, "friends," social contacts, professional associations, material possessions and numerous other soft entities that cooperate to enshrine the myth of our specialness to life. Even so, this image is plainly an imposter that interposes an illusion in place of our reality. We are duped into believing our original face is the leper in the room and a countenance far too terrifying to every look at in the eye. Thus our carbon copy outward appearance is architected to precision and it serves as a buffer that veils the raw truth about ourselves. In consequence, we spend many hapless lives behind this flimsy facade, deceiving ourselves and others.

Some feel empty and hollow inside, and they attempt to compensate for their deficiencies by engaging the old-time illusions of power and destruction. Thus they propagate meaningless wars and lose no chance to escalate violence and conflict. Still, no outward limit of power can soften or assuage the absolute tyranny, they crave. All-out nuclear war does not go far enough towards satiating the hunger of their inner beast. Others are so self-hateful and consumed with rage that they perpetuate endless cycles of abuse, vandalism, torture, extortion, and neglect. They steer well clear of peace and its minions because seen in the calm, serene mirror of existential purity; their cruel intentions would stand too brutally exposed. All mischievous thoughts not acted out immediately will be vicariously dramatized later on by making a nightly trip to the local S&M club.

Now meet the chronically worthless, whose worlds must always be brimming to overflow with a dazzling panorama of fanciful toys and VIPs. They prowl and scavenge the universe for all external surrogates who can magnify and aggrandize their lofty self-perception. Unable to face their internal deficiencies, they head out in their high-cost rags and sports cars into that sickening halo of nauseating pomp and grandeur. Not for them, the raw mystical wisdom and equanimity of the Buddha because they have looked within and found nothing there, but a moth-eaten scarecrow. Instead, they will snort their way up the angel dust highway, in search of some soul-crushing party. Perhaps, to the house of a celebrity high in the hills where they may find a haven, at last, in which to expound their nauseating opinions to some broken down octogenarian who is about ready to kick the bucket. Their delight is in saturating the airwaves with juicy tales of world-shattering conspiracies; then passionately sputtering on a variety of topics ranging from misinformation wars to the local dirty laundry. Nonetheless, all is but an umbral compensation designed to obfuscate the naked banality of their humdrum existence.

Those who live the lie of their invented self-image are incapable of discerning value in themselves and others. This self-conjured image serves as a shield against an underlying conviction of worthlessness. A life of deception is all we can expect from one who continuously engages the black arts of trickery and pretense. Truth becomes impossible for all who have conned, hoodwinked and entrapped so enthusiastically since birth. Their distortive mind frame bars the gates of their consciousness to all that is luminous and real.

It is most assuredly a world run by those wearing masks and those who indulge in various superficial modes of communication. Behind these masks lies a torrent of all that is impure, perverse and meaningless. It is an unholy deluge that forever cuts life, from life and it is there in all the elitist groups, wealth clubs, and enclaves of specialness that populate the modern landscape. All those systems of entitlement that carve deep in our collective psyche. From these are forged all our insidious hierarchies, social orders, class distinctions and repressive structures of segregation. Hence the middle class becomes easily manipulated into being a piggy bank for the oligarchs and wealthy. Then the sheep are promptly garnished and served on a platter.

The same cancerous virus has rapidly spread into all our professional organizations, universities, workplaces, sports venues and entertainment industries. The universal caste system is just one more system of specialness intro- duced by the ego. It remains a sham and outright injustice because there can be no caste, in what is One. All artificial monstrosities of insincerity in the world are hatched through a pervasive mindless coercion, which forces each to adopt some false image. Our hypocrisy and complicity stacks the deck against us, and our thinly disguised veneer precludes all collaborative progress towards more primal interests. Those who know not, the Self, stumble out into Avatarville, to purchase a mask of their liking before all are sold-out. It seems, no one can afford to stand idly by, naked and exposed. Even so, not knowing the Self, how can they ever rightly appraise what is worthy and to be treasured? Thus this never-ending costume party will go on until the realization dawns it is a ruse—a game played against yourself in which the house always wins. Whenever we choose deception over self-honesty, we always lose.

THE MYTH OF NORMALCY

The wealth and power accumulation games offered by psychoplanet have always been rigged in favor of those competently skilled in sophistry, manipulation, and deceit. Such materialistic, superficial beings who know how to adapt well and bend the rules are what society considers "normal." The worldly-wise and socially ambitious, who sell themselves daily for the gifts of the marketplace are esteemed as the sanest members of our social fabric. Highly sensitive creative souls, in contrast, are often denounced, as poorly adjusted, then rapidly labeled weird, isolationist or even as non-compos mentis. They can recognize the carnage and brutality, and all those tricks people play to dissimulate and victimize. Additionally, they see through all our masks, conflicting desires, and fleeting ambitions. Regrettably, they may lack the transcendental insight needed to exit this show. Being unable to conform they soon find themselves at an insurmountable impasse, and it's one that can tear their psyche to shreds.

Our conception of normal has become wholly twisted. It consists of those base creatures whose minds are always brimming with ten-thousand competing desires and those who can quickly habituate to a world of insanity. One's entire lack of Self-knowledge, core integrity, and moral fiber does not seem to matter. Once you lose all interest in nursing vain and futile desires, you fall off the wagon. To stare blankly outward dispassionately at everyone swiftly induces angry reactions and fear. No! You must have your life-script, up and running, or hide away in some asylum. Nonetheless, the glaring fact remains that those most split and disintegrated within are likely to be very comfortable wearing masks and the best suited for sauntering elegantly on the many catwalks of life! This system of normalcy is entirely delusional. Just take away any one of their special toys or merits, for an instant, and you will see them quickly unraveling before you. It seems their very precarious balloon has suddenly gone pop and so they experience a breakdown. It can be an absolute and irrevocable meltdown with no recovery in sight because all straws of their sanity are so tightly coupled with their attachments. They have no insight into their fundamental reality, at a higher level. At the collective level, the crucial issue of not knowing who we Are gives rise to numerous group psychoses. The projected manifestation of our underlying psychotic condition is witnessed in all our witch-hunts, persecutions, genocides, wars, blacklists, international espionage, double-dealings, misinformation campaigns to name but a few.

WHY PSYCHOTHERAPY DOES NOT WORK!

Modern psychotherapeutic methods are for the most part wholly ineffective. The unveiling process at the level of the intellect is only capable of delivering temporary psychological Band-Aids and quick-fix solutions, but it elicits no lasting cure. Unfrocking long-buried skeletons to find evidence of past traumas, latent motives, carefully concealed intentions and personality deficiencies cannot heal unless these can be readily eradicated and dismissed. Psychotherapy's highest aspiration is to have us conform to an insane world, rather than transcend it. Meanwhile, the real roots of our problems go unresolved, and our inner Buddhas remain blissfully slumbering. Only the Vision bestowed by perfect knowledge and compassion knows with certainty that this relative world is void. The dominant focus of psychotherapy, however, is exploring the lower mind of the ego, and it makes no attempt to disavow the world of appearances. It works exclusively on our self-defenses, worldly reactions and behaviors rather than penetrating through to the underlying cause of our misery.

Knowing full well just how vicious and capricious, the ego can be and believing it has reality, psychotherapists dare not adventure to the other side of the mask. They are more interested in sedating the patient with neuroleptics and inhibiting their higher functional modes and critical thinking capacities, than in revealing the real source of their angst. The message is clear, "*No one is paid enough dollars to fumigate your inner demons.*" Their powerlessness to heal is because their entire emphasis is on darkness. However, analyzing darkness affirms it has reality. Healing, on the other hand, depends on removing all barriers to light. The elimination of self-made obstacles is the only efficacious approach for restoring lasting sanity and peace. Healing derives from reaching the life-giving fountainhead within. Once we fearlessly adventure to the other side of the dark cloud we made, all our anxieties and futile sufferings will subside and disappear. They are born out of our reactive responses to a shifting and volatile world that we fail to take ownership for. One cannot reach unconditional peace apart from the world or within it but only it recognizing its essential unreality. This is accomplished by no longer projecting fearful thoughts and interpretations.

Unfortunately, many psychotherapists begin the healing process closed-minded to the real possibilities. Their fundamental thesis is that no lasting mental health is probable, or feasible for a mind haunted by so many demons! They interpret it as a perpetual battlefield, something akin to *Lord of the Rings*. A nebulous place in which so many chimerical beasts roam about, filled with rage and confusion. Their failure is in recognizing, that all such incubi, idle fantasies, defenses, and distortions arose due to the absence of light. Alternatively, they may interpret your mind-frame as a minefield, laden with uncertainty and risk. So one poorly delivered word or thought could potentially set off a bouncing betty, resulting in a relapse, meltdown or suicide. Their whole effort and investment, therefore, is in making a better adjustment to your mask; not uncovering your fundamental issues. This therapeutic approach is a case of the blind leading the blind, but they are the ones holding the prescription book.

FINDING OUR AUTHENTIC BEING

Unless you are willing and ready to reach your pure innermost Being, you live a goalless existence. Perhaps, it is time to sign up as an organ donor, and end it quickly, rather than continue to photocopy your mediocrity for all to see. Yes, surrendering to a quick death is probably a far more noble act than plagiarizing the thoughts and behaviors of other beings. Most live carnivorously off the flesh of the mob and media, and this is the exact opposite of living fearlessly, adventurously and authentically. Enormous damage arises whenever we parade the spectacle of our ignorance and cross-contaminate it to other minds. It feeds the contagion of our collective deception and misdirects many down painful and abortive paths. The solution for restoring awareness of our Identity breaks down principally to two critical processes:

(1) Information

(2) Communication

INFORMATION

Information can be powerful, but it can also be highly destructive. It possesses an exceedingly broad spectrum, and whether we like it or not, we are immersed in a world consisting of many different categories of information. Certain types of information are pernicious and malicious, and even poisonous. They can be used to bring down corporations, governments, to malign or even to send one to jail for life. Another class of information is simply wasteful of one's time. Every day we are bombarded with tons of useless information, including spam, marketing adds, phishing e-mails and media attempts to brainwash our thought patterns. There is also a very potent strain of information that serves to empower, free, enliven, heal and bless. Discerning and filtering out that tiny fraction which is useful, is an art in itself. Lacking wise guidance from within most will continuously throw the baby out with the bathwater. Many mindtools can help us to evaluate valuable information from the destructive or worthless. These tools include Reason, Induction, Analogy, Inference, Intuition and Past Experiences.

Information shapes our thoughts, values, experiences, and identities. The convoluted matrix of our beliefs crystallizes from both **(1)** the information we have received and **(2)** how we have interpreted it. Beliefs are the Himalayas of the mind. They frame our perception, configure our thought processes, motivate our choices and decisions and influence what experiences we will engage. All we seek to do or avoid derives from our tenaciously held convictions. Our beliefs determine what friends we will attract, clubs and affiliations we will join, careers and professions we will embrace, and they impress deeply upon our emotional world, character and psychological states. A lot is hanging in the balance. Our entire success and failure depend on our ability to sort and act on the information we receive. No thought or decision is ever neutral in its effects. Even an idea, conception or theory that may appear bland at the surface, will either lead to what is extremely meaningful and liberating or else it will imprison. Each one of our thoughts encapsulates some fundamental content which is either true or fallacious. No idea exists in isolation. Each connects to a vast array of other thoughts and ideas, whose forms may appear different on the surface but whose content remains the same.

Self-Realization is no accident. Wisdom dawns only when one is ripe. Those who mature and blossom know how to separate reliably and consistently the treasurable from the trash. It is gutsy pioneers exclusively who reach the Everest of true understanding because these matchless ones will never uphold second-hand opinion in place of first-hand knowledge. Unless you have known something directly at your core, it remains just superficial knowledge. Self-Realization flowers spontaneously once you undertake a fearless odyssey past all shadowy and ambiguous thought-formations that occlude the light of Truth and knowledge of Spirit. On this bountiful and worthwhile expedition, rigorous and indiscriminate self-inquiry will be your guide to dispel all false knowledge.

To begin the adventure, you must first consciously decide to deceive yourself no longer. We lie to ourselves profusely, and this is a leading source of interference. Our rationalizations, justifications, oversimplifications, and economies of truth are major impediments to our advancement. They dampen our will and tarnish our objectivity and impartiality. We all prefer and will graciously swallow the convenient lie over an inconvenient truth any day. You must cease to be persuaded and distracted by various temptations, whimsical notions, flimsy one-dimensional assertions, shallow conceptualizations and toxic ideational patterns. Soon, you will experience progress and see all your identity problems, instabilities and conflicting behaviors begin to melt and disappear. Finally you will reach to certitude and enjoy unconditional peace at last.

Until you choose to be Master over your thought, your thought will rule over you. Whenever you hand over your only seat of power, the consequences are always disastrous. Taking no responsibility for your mind forces all your thoughts, moods, behaviors, actions and decisions to be at the mercy of unruly impressions and unsound conceptions. Your perception will soon transform into a twisted maelstrom of capricious happenings and fearful images, and you will appear to wander as a lonely stray dog in an arid and vengeful landscape, feeling lost and isolated and hopelessly enveloped in a sickened tomb.

The ego will never clue you in on the true cost of your masks of deception because it needs your continued investment in them to prop up the mirage of its own existence. Hence, it persuades and brainwashes, that all your pretenses, biases, partialities and misunderstandings have no price and that your closed-mindedness, bigotry, fanaticism and prejudice work in your favor. It desires you be hyper-vigilant in maintaining all its defenses and instruments of attack because doing so, it slyly obstructs access to your Whole Being and thus prevents healing. It does not matter if you live in a beautiful palace if all the rooms are hermetically sealed, and you are powerless to roam about. To esteem, any mask is to endorse a world of falseness, insincerity, and superficiality over your serene and potent reality. So you enter a world of illusions and become condemned to wastefully spending your entire life in some tiny cobweb infested enclave, down near the dungeons.

The ego likes to convince you that time is your friend and that you can dilly-dally and vacillate as much as you like and still make excellent progress. Time, however, is just like a bank account, in which you are unaware of your remaining balance. One day you will go to withdraw some more time, only to find you are in the red. That is the day you will die! Many spend their whole lives working their tails off on nonsense crap. They seem to delight in procrastinating and busying themselves with non-essentials. They fail to capitalize on the immense treasure they have been given this moment; a golden opportunity to find freedom, truth, and peace. The chance to authentically live now and be transformed. Whether you decide wisely or not, the exact instant your account will become overdrawn is already predetermined. Lamentably foolish people project their lifespan based on the actuarial tables for life expectancy. They never let it sink in that they may be one of the outliers or fringe data points of high deviation.

You may ask, *"How I do evaluate the quality of any thought or piece of information?"* The answer is deceptively simple. The qualitative value of all real information is always of the same order. The concept "more" information is meaningless in Eternity. In the paradisiacal kingdom of the timeless, content alone is all that matters. This antipodal emphasis is what differentiates it from worldly knowledge, and it realigns with what is tremendously potent and creative. Real information is always true, as opposed to conditionally true. It is not subject to the vagaries of time but is always radiant and certain. You will either understand and appreciate the content wholly or not at all. To understand it, is to become it and once it is thoroughly imbibed and assimilated, you become incredibly joyous. At that moment, you become free of the world of time. Then you readily purge all illusions, contradictions and self-destructive thoughts that have infiltrated your mind, since time began. True information always brings life in its wake; never-ending streams of vitality, tremendous healing that a purity that is uncontainable. Now you see the limitless potency of what started off as a mere seed and recognize the power in essence.

COMMUNICATION

Communication is life! Once we are bereft of a means of communication; we become effectively dead. Relegated to living our lives in a test tube or as some brain bathing in a jar of acid. Communication is pivotal for clarifying our understandings and refining our beliefs, and it is primal to our continued evolution and growth. When we devote ourselves to teaching falsities, we attract and reinforce such nonsense in our minds. The outcome is a perpetual muddle-headed confusion and a severely dissociated condition. Unwisely, we expend the bulk of our energy and time communicating that our "separated" condition is real. By using countless names and classifications, we indoctrinate and imbue all with the fallacy that they are separate and independent entities. Consequently, we remain profoundly split and confused and live under the delusion of inhabiting an object-orientated existence. Our Whole Mind has become fractured and dissociated into billions of different aspects, all seemingly housed in separate bodies. We now lack the knowledge that we are unified and One and that each of us is a critical piece of a spectacular heavenly jigsaw puzzle of trans-cosmic proportions. Taken from a holistic perspective, each aspect of mind possesses the perfect understanding of Whole-Mind.

Whole-Mind alone is the Home of Pure Knowledge because individual aspects always distort. In consequence, we generate illusions that shroud the Real and so lose access to unadulterated wisdom. Knowledge can only be regained through our perfect integration. This unifying synthesis heals our experience of split-mind and removes all illusions. It is a process that occurs in time because from the towering vantage point of the Eternal; we have always remained Whole and gleam everlastingly in immaculate splendor.

The profound dissociation, known as "**split-mind**" can be considered an extreme form of multiple personality disorder (**MPD**). Each aspect of Mind retains the Totality of Knowledge, but this becomes lost to awareness, due to the interference of ego toxicity. The ego functions as a jamming device, and it garbles every message. Its senseless drivel and chatter conditions our minds to be in ceaseless conflict. Thus we remain hounded by existential paradoxes, meaninglessness, and endless contradictions until we can harness the right insights needed to free ourselves. Until then our thought processes will be implacably swamped and suffused with worldly thoughts.

Our self-concept arises as an ego defense mechanism against Truth. Each such concept is entirely based on false premises and represents the ego's pitiless attempt to restore wholeness through entertaining illusions and false images. For this is its supreme plan of salvation! It is impossible, however, to patch our way back to Wholeness and Divine Wisdom, by worshipping idols, nourishing special relationships and esteeming the worthless. We merely embark on a series of wild, reckless and harebrained misadventures to find meaning in the meaningless. Our continuous state of misery, anxiety, and angst must surely be a clear sign that this strategy is not working!

TUNING IN

Communication is bidirectional. So optimizing and tuning our capacities to receive can be far more important than all those confused messages and self-marketing hype we continuously broadcast. An open mind draws enlightened wisdom to itself. It attracts subtle and esoteric knowledge beyond the scope of all perceived worlds. This wisdom can only reveal itself through the inner eyes of our intuition and mystical vision. It bypasses all our faulty understandings and remains serenely unclouded by all our biases, prejudices and self-induced limitations. In this luminous all-encompassing manifold, everyone is made welcome, and each situation is accepted for what it is. Every moment, the unseen universe is speaking its words of wisdom into our ears, but can we hear them? No! Our minds have erected too many barriers and defenses and these function as the prison-house which limits our capacities to receive. Have you ever noticed how selective and misplaced your perceptions can be and how lukewarm, narrow-banded and rigor mortis your beliefs?

We all forge a perceptual filter that will only accept what we are willing to see and hear. So we place sentinels on our senses that automatically exclude and obfuscate. What our mind find unattractive is deemphasized and lost. How many times, have you refused wisdom from the tongue of an unworthy one? How often have you signed off on a mammoth pile of hogwash from one, you highly esteem? We are disgusted when wisdom is expounded from a form we find distasteful. Most will embrace only the opinions, insights and sagacity of those with whom they wish to develop special relationships. Those who protect their primary thought system, ideologies and belief structures are welcomed and no one else.

The Holy Spirit's Voice and Message speaks through all tongues at once. Unless we are open to hearing it everywhere, we will not hear it at all. Communication is crucial to our well-being and health. As we communicate honestly and boundlessly, we restore awareness of our real Identity. Perfect understanding precipitates from no longer communicate self-made distortions and lies. We leverage our communication capacities most effectively by directing them both inward and outward. As we intra-communicate and intercommunicate competently we flourish.

INTRA-COMMUNICATION

Intra-communication is a powerful means of mending and invigorating our lives. We improve our life quality, whenever we reinterpret and heal the fundamental thought processes that drive it. The intra-communication of our endogenous thoughts and beliefs through introspection both disempowers and frees us of all internal demons. Directing our communication probes inward and downward, much as a bat uses sonar, to investigate our underlying psychology and belief structures is liberating. This is a therapeutic journey, in which we analyze, clarify and reorganize that which we know. Over time, our mind becomes extremely proficient at watching itself, and its core thought processes and this releases all false and unproven knowledge and our misplaced identifications. We reach clarity to the extent that we resolve all thought contradictions and uncover new insights and perspectives. Our healing and self-purification soon become reflected in our changed behaviors and increased peacefulness and beatitude. During moments of deep introspection, the very foundation of our metaphysical understanding becomes rigorously exposed and starts to tear apart. The true relationship between ourselves and the world becomes known. Dismantling all that is false induces meaningful transformation, and the ultimate pinnacle of this activity is Enlightenment.

In a single instant; your entire self-concept can be vaporized; seen as just home-grown fiction projected into the world. Once this fictional bubble becomes subsumed and submerged, all boundaries and self-inventions disappear, and your supreme reality is known. Then you become capable of perfect communication with the entire ocean of Mind and attain **Absolute Bodhicitta**. You arrive at the perfection of knowledge. The belief system which forges the Relative World is seen through at last and promptly disavowed. As all illusory partitions and separations fabricated out of ignorance dissolve, you enter the formless existence.

INTERCOMMUNICATION

Intercommunication is a synergistic hybridization of two essential processes, namely: **(1) Communication** and **(2) Interaction**. Through it, we strengthen and refine our primary understandings and knowledge-base by communicating them freely with all. The principal intention is to expand and transmogrify our flashes of insight by purifying them in the fire of another mind. This directs us on a course that is the exact opposite of being pig-headed, closed-off and seeking to enforce our nonsense opinions. The pivotal recognition is that **Truth can never attack and can never be attacked.** Knowing this, we gladly entrust our ideas and understandings to all and welcome the fact, that if they are found fraudulent or false, they can be promptly rescinded or denounced. Exposing them functions as a gift to ourselves since it relinquishes our bondage to the fallacious. If they are weeds, that strangle and poison our thought, they are unworthy of our minds. Similarly, if they are found valuable and true, we will learn to treasure them and put them to greater use. Over time through positive feedback, we become empowered to develop their potential, and so open new doors and vistas of being.

No sane mind sees value in separation. Such a mind will never promote attacks nor circulate divisive, judgmental and condemnatory rhetoric. It will not air its grievances, nor waste time pointing out weaknesses, faults or sins in others. Since its only goal is healing, its one desire is to increase integration. In its goal of peace, it strives to be more forgiving and compassionate, knowing this is the path also to greater stability and strength. Soon, it recognizes its invulnerability and comprehends the world was never against it. The only enemy was its confusion of thought and this confusion was self-generated. The world of perception then gladly reciprocates and gives a perfect response to its progressive intentions. All distortionary aspects of perception begin disappearing as we reintegrate. Soon we gain access to the inner radiance which we impeded before through all our judgments, misunderstandings and grievances. Then the inner light gushes outward illuminating a new world. Our entire path forward has been revealed as is our complete release from hell. We comprehend very viscerally, the timeless truth: *"As within, so without"* and fathom, that there can be no *"within"* or *"without"* in that which is forever unified. Truth has no direction since it exists everywhere, and always, as the supreme underlying pure essence of all. All illusions of difference, distance and separation soon give way, and the inner and outer worlds merge and transcend all artificial boundaries, which seemed so imposing before. The vital recognition is cognizing that there is no "other" and no self and that the illusion of otherness only arose due to our projection of aspects of our thought.

This path of intercommunication is one in which we can attain **Relative Bodhicitta**. In an epiphany, we intuit that all problems of identity arose from communicating the false. Living in denial leads to further dissociation and strengthens our split-mind. Hence, a false identity is empowered to flourish and mature in the weeds of the world. Communication of what is true and veracious leads to life. Mind knows itself, based on the quality of what it communicates. Whenever our communication becomes broken, limited or infiltrated with falsities, our identity problems escalate. Consequently, we begin to feel disconnected and alienated. At the individual level, this results in the proliferation of various psychoses, particularly schizophrenia and MPD. Whenever we communicate false notions, we strengthen them, in both ourselves and "others." In consequence, the dream soon descends into darkness, and we experience unnecessary suffering and despair. When we communicate only partially, the cleansing of our beliefs and ideas is retarded, and our minds become blocked to a supremely radiant wisdom. The effects of poor communication are overtly manifest everywhere in the world. At the collective level, it includes various pandemics, group hallucinations, stock market crashes and over-attachment to old patterns of defensive thinking. The body is another example of a collective belief that unfortunately became shared. Even though it is a phantom, it is continuously reinforced because of our chronic and profound state of dissociation.

THE SCARCITY BELIEF

The scarcity belief is rampant in the Relative World. Our conviction in underlying scarcity automatically directs all our decisions and actions. It puts us in a chronic state of anxiety and apprehension because we are afraid the bare essentials will become too costly and healthcare too expensive. As we look out the stain streaked window at the old junker we cannot afford to repair, we feel ourselves to be vulnerable minions. Consequently, it does not take much for us to become extremely fearful and outright vicious. Gradually, we begin to silently endorse the universal belief in scarcity and start proclaiming we live on a planet with limited resources. We are heard shouting from the rooftops that there is only so much clean water, food, natural resources, and precious metals, etc. to go around. The dismal setting becomes reinforced by "glowing" news reports that bombard us daily with dark tales portending the rape and depletion of our world by rapacious, selfish and unscrupulous interests.

Our ears feast on such stories. They describe in stunning detail how a certain country is hoarding the global inventory of a rare and precious metal, while another is stockpiling all the Gold reserves. Meanwhile, a few others are secretly conspiring to monopolize all the oil and gas supplies. Legions of stories leak depicting China in very stygian colors and painting it as some mongrel crossbreed of Ebenezer Scrooge and Dorian Gray. The dark silhouette portrayed, powerfully depicts its illicit engagement in black market activity while brazenly launching programs of industrial espionage. There are ruminations of how it is fervently supporting various guerrilla factions and bandits and furnishing them with Kalashnikovs so that they can head out to dehorn all the Rhinos and dehusk all the elephants.

Even a fake media report full of baseless speculation can send stock prices skyrocketing or sharply plunging. Such reports are designed to massage the markets intentionally and in the interests of a select minority. It seems all the *Chicken Littles* in the statistical and number crunching professions need to justify their paychecks. So they blitz us with an avalanche of statistical charts, which convincingly project the world's alarming rate of population growth. The picture is so bleak we are informed that if enough people do the *Cha-Cha in* Borneo, the Earth will rapidly spin out of orbit and go whirling like a comet into the great unknown.

It is not long before all these tales seep down in the vast reservoirs of our subconscious and begin cranking the engines of fear into action. Soon everyone starts to feel the pinch and buys into the myth that there are not enough resources to go around. In the consequent delirium, we start having nightmares about enforced Euthanasia and about having to eat *Soylent Green*. It is only natural that we collectively project our fear, hate, and suspicions to other nations. The smaller countries, we simply ignore or begin to treat like lepers—something akin to the original settlers arriving at Ellis Island. Maybe we just give them a few sharp jabs under the ribs before kicking them in the underbelly. Then for dessert, we proceed to manipulate and slaughter their currencies and place them in perpetual debt and surrogacy to our banking system. Don't we love our magical institutions of financial wizardry, who can conjure up cash from thin air, like rabbits from a hat! However, it is our retirement accounts that go down the flusher when they are forced to fold and withdraw from the game of universal poker.

We take a more bullying stance with larger nations. We begin the party by announcing our intention to erect thirty-foot walls to keep all outcasts and lowlifes out. We place all the debt as lies on the piggy bank of the middle-class because we want to break their backs and subjugate them. Now it is time to up the stakes, and so we begin jockeying for a strategic position in the international ecosystem. Proudly we point to the giant phallus of our nuclear weapons and aim it square in the forehead of another nation. I think our secret goal to the rip out the inner eye of their Shiva Netra. Yes, it is a nasty cocktail, this political Mai Tai, and it is one full of noxious ingredients including BS, sweat, and pungent testosterone, but nothing can taste as rancid as our raw hate, tasted through the sieve of our cultivated civility. Then we enact a ban on Burkas, Turbans, and Hijabs at all our airports. Now it is time to start deporting innocents en masse and slicing families into pieces. Of course, all this has nothing to with a particular race, sect or nation but rather aimed to fumigate a growing lice infection. All of which sends the temperature of our collective cauldron intensifying towards a full-blown meltdown.

BALANCING THE SCALES

The law of scarcity is a core law by which the ego survives and thrives in our mind. Without it, it could never tempt us into unsolicited attacks, born from our fears of poverty and lack. The ego enjoys singing into our ears, endless lullabies which preach of our material wealth deficiencies. They start out like this:

"Whatever one possesses or steals, it is always at the expense of another. It is inevitable that some must starve so that others can eat well. Someone must be the beggar so that you can enjoy the high life. All nations are voracious in their never-ending needs to pillage and plunder and doing so they deprive us all. Our failure is imminent unless we rapidly stockpile our way to success. We do not want to end as a slave nation, shining the Master's shoes while paying exorbitant interest on our national debt to some rogue outfit."

These tacit unspoken beliefs are a leading cause of all wars. In fact, they are used to rationalize them. We like to think of wars as conscientiously invoked after much deliberation or that they are acts of justly deserved retaliation. However, the real seeds of international warfare are greed, religion, and various pernicious ideologies. Anyone who is well-fed and well-taken care off doesn't give a rat's ass about initiating war. As you may well expect, the ego's belief in scarcity is an essential cornerstone of its overall philosophy, and it helps foster and cement intractable beliefs in our "victimhood." After all, if we are at the mercy of the external world of things, how can we be divine beings and possessors of the limitless?

No! We must be extremely vigilant, or we will be left at the bottom of the food chain, cleaning the mansions of the wealthy, in our later years. We must save ourselves, first and foremost, then extricate ourselves from this ship of madness. Let's seduce our way into some cushy position and become the manipulators instead of the manipulated. Because when the music stops and world economies crash and burn, and cyber attacks, inflation, and extortion are widespread, we will need a cushion to avoid the piles. Otherwise, we will end up, as some minion in a factory, with a crocked body, and failing mind while paid a dime for every ton of sweat hours.

All who view the perceived universe, as the ultimate reality must worship this law of scarcity. This is because, from every angle, it callously mocks God's Laws of Justice and

Abundance. Those who confidently proclaim this world, as their higher power must see God as completely absent from the greater equation of their lives. Perhaps, He has lost the edge as well as the savoir-faire and cunning needed to keep up with the sub-nanosecond trading. Maybe, it is high-time, he became decommissioned as a power and needs to be relegated now to some stockroom boy in some modern corporate empire.

Darwinian survival of the fittest is the name of the game we like most to indulge. In the final analysis, all happenings and events here on psychoplanet are nothing but sublimated Anarchy. This is a dish made barely palatable by the devious icing of convoluted, legalistic jargon that conceals its sour taste. Opportunism is a dream only for the super-rich. There to empower the Oligarchs and plutocracies and all who can afford the legions of duplicitous lawyers who can speak through forked tongues 24x7. Certainly, civility is only a garment the wealthy get to wear and enjoy, but it works against the rest of us. While we lay meekly down to sleep, to have our nightmares of scarcity, the wolves of Wall Street are out stealing our dinner in the great Casinos of the world. Casinos that have always been rigged in the interests of the bosses.

No mind functions in a vacuum and no one lives without placing their stake somewhere. We automatically invest our chips wherever we perceive the greatest ROI. It will be either in the worldly or the transcendental because these are the only real options in town. Rationalizations always come later. Will it be then in the idols of the stock market, and the many games of money manipulation property acquisition that promise some measure of power, status, and class on the worldly stage? Or in cyber-snooping our way to notoriety through the crafting of malicious homegrown software? Perhaps, you believe the lie of getting an edge through a good education? We all will gladly devote our lives towards worshipping a massive pile of dung if only it will grant us some favors. Chronic normalcy and mediocrity are the highways to nowhere. They cannot even provide a living wage. Instead, they send us careening down the slippery slopes into economic poverty traps, financial ruin and the mud-pit of diminishing prospects. Let's take our chances while we can because the doomsday prophet is about to blow his trumpet. Let's jump in naked into the pleasure pits and cesspools of this world rather than bathe in the noxious pool of our mediocrity. Let's extract some temporary satisfaction, at the very least, and do our morning ululations to Bacchus while bidding the Pharaohs of the modern age farewell. Adieu then to Gates, Jobs, Brin, and Zuckerberg! Let not their portals and cyber-pyramids to the Sun God turn us all into Nexus 6 zombies.

It must be evident, by now, that scarcity is a universal belief pervading the world. It insidious presence has companies at each other's throats, and Nations pitted against Nation. Each wants to be top dog in the show, even if this involves gutting and disemboweling the innards of their neighbors and loved ones. Collaboration is a word for the weak and defenseless. One, never to be whispered by a superpower such as the great US of A. Instead, we need to hint delicately at war and Armageddon while brandishing our whips and swords around the world—though dumb-fuck is not so softspoken.

We need to start the engines in the lower chambers and horsewhip those Black Shoe Engineers back to work so that they continue to burn the midnight oil for our national treasury. Maybe flatter them with a nice meal and a hotel room for a night, then tell them it's good riddance to their family, health and work-life balance for over a decade. Let them do their time in solitary out in the open and to the deafening sound of tyrannical managers who will smack each with a cane over the knuckles, in an instant. It is either that or time spent in the gutter and a lifetime of dumpster diving, eating Top Ramen and living out of a storage locker.

Who gives a damn about freedom of information and full disclosure? Such beautiful lofty concepts, but ultimately useful only for misty-eyed dreamers! Remember, our lawyers are paid well for a reason. They are there to steal our inventions, do damage mitigation, avoid taxes and engage in hostile takeovers. Why else do you think we are so focused on industrial espionage, reverse engineering and subjugating the indigenous sheep in our factories? What will be the future of your startup? Will it emit that vibrant crackly sound of a cockroach as it crunches into overnight obsolescence under the heathen's foot? The success of fledgling companies, we consider unconditionally seditious to our oligarchical dictatorship. We bet against them, just like the Dodo bird. We plan they will never get off the ground and soon go extinct. Then we will sleep well in our monopoly induced comas.

The ego's fundamental creed is to possess just for the sake of possession. Endless accumulation and hoarding is the goal and the prevalent attitude, characteristic of all of the separated ones, even those whose needs are all met, a million times over. Unfortunately, the ego sees its value in direct proportion to its number of trophies it has or heads stringing on a nylon over the fire in its grand mansion. Who cares if all the toys are stored away in the garage are never used because all will be held spellbound by the endless arrays of stuffed animals in the foyer, rare paintings on the walls and vintage wines in the cellar. A ravenous, wanton and limitless appetite is the only infinity the ego can ever conceive because its belly is always empty and no glory can suffice. It does not believe in working for the common good but only in seducing those more powerful. For it is always in need of more jewels and gemstones stringing around its neck. To this insufferable hall of pomp and glory, where there is nothing but blind extortion and fear, the Course comes to our rescue. It defiantly announces that our universe is merely one of ideas and proclaims that we do not live in the world; rather it lives in us! We do not need to entertain, any wild fear of things running out or of planetary rape and destruction. All that is perceived is but the projection of concepts in our mind. This profound understanding undoes all fearful premises at their foundation and all which fuels our convictions of scarcity, So, there is no world of rare metals and oil reserves that can ever be depleted. Material things are all ego projections, and all forms and images are fabricated from its neurotic distortions. For no form could ever contain the limit-less, and no image can symbolize the infinitely potent.

"*But what about my body?*" You meekly inquire as you wit-ness it becoming more worn down, pressure cooked and tired by the day. The Course responds: *It has never been there and exists only as a reflection of our thoughts. It will appear to be reborn until you transcend those limited thought patterns that bring it into pseudo-being.* Thus fear loses one of its dominant mainsprings, by which it clings for survival in your thought. A single shaft of light and hope has entered your barren world—one that heralds complete emancipation from foolish beliefs. This light-ray over time will integrate and harmonize your mind thor-oughly with the Laws of Truth. Now spirit speaks to willing ears about the universal and immutable **Law of Abun-dance.** A Law, nonetheless which only the wise and altru-istic know how to apply effectively to the realm of percep-tion. Spirit teaches, that ideas are strengthened by being shared and how all is an idea. You cannot, therefore, lose by giving, but can only gain. Blessing all and extending profusely is the way to know of your abundance and wholeness. More succinctly put, "*The means to know you already Are all.*" Hence its emphasis on, **"To Have. Give All to All" [T-6.V.A]** as the first lesson.

VICTIMHOOD

O ur attraction to victimhood is immense. Each day we are tempted to cry out the sad tale of our victimization to anyone, who will listen. Every time, we utter a grievance we are declaring our victimhood to the world. Our compromised position is also betrayed by our anger, fear, cynicism, threatening behaviors and general aura of discontent. Many fall into the endless abyss of victimhood for lifetimes and never reemerge. We can recognize these tragic figures all around. We see them in the bars, silently crying in their pints or else outside the supermarkets holding up some sign. Some never budge from their apartments and undertake no new adventures and prefer instead to surround themselves with a dizzying array of meaningless things. Some drag themselves into the workplace and try to hide their acute feelings of victimization under the flimsy veil of frenzied activity.

Many start out in life confident and brimming with optimism. However, after a few setbacks bitterness can set in and a day arrives when we all feel tempted to declare our victimhood. It will probably be on that day when you have fallen on hard times and are in the jaws of despair. Perhaps, your Doctor has just informed you, that you have an incurable disease or maybe you find yourself drowning in insurmountable debt. Alternatively, you may have had an epiphany, and recognize the sheer meaninglessness of your life. In an instant, you fathom life's incontestable staleness and perceive it for the moth ridden prison-house, which it is. Immediately, an emptiness creeps into your soul, and you get that unquenchable, lonely feeling of total isolation. One that makes you shake to the bone. Then, in desperation, you reach out to communicate and vent before you crack. So you speed-dial some friends a dozen times or more but get no response. A part of you is stunned and unable to fathom the callousness of humanity. Worse still, you hear a dry, dispassionate voice crackling at the other end of the phone that sounds so cold and unsympathetic. It sends shivers down your spine. You feel duped and know this particular alliance is ended. Just like all ego contracts, they soon become insolvent, once the repayment terms become too steep.

Our belief in our interminable crucifixion by an unstable and insane world leads each to have intense feelings of anxiety, insecurity, and vulnerability. The threat of impending abandonment can amplify our fears to extreme proportions. It can make us feel powerless, trashy and ea-

ger to please, even to the point of being outright posses-
sive, suffocating and insufferable to be around. The tiniest
incident can incense us at a visceral level. So the flames of
fear flare up and soon manifest as uncontrollable rage! Anything is liable to happen now. Your breathing patterns
change, and your body language becomes filled with intim-
idation. Then searing streams of malicious intent shoot out
from your eyeballs like death-rays, and your mind becomes twisted with sad tales of its perpetual torment and
injustice. Blinded by all your self-serving agendas, and defenses your intemperate fury functions as fuel on the af-
terburner. Then as the insatiable monster turns inward,
you experience overwhelming depression and bitterness.
Your hostile attitudes and behaviors soon betray the caustic lacerations engraved in your heart.

The attraction of victimhood is a dominant pillar of the
ego's thought and remains a prime psychological mechanism by which it continuously leverages itself. Your commitment to this strange belief furnishes the ego with all the
ammunition, it needs, to secure many "evils" into place. It
loves to preach how it is always you against the world and
how your bare survival depends on becoming aggressive,
cunning, slippery and deceitful. You must take care of *nu-
mero uno* at all time because friends will quickly depart

when it becomes too inconvenient. They will seek better pastures as soon as you can no longer wine-and-dine them or be of value. Many who have felt this sting become overnight sell-outs and rapidly morph into cold-hearted opportunists who prey on all. Dead to themselves and having eviscerated all love, altruism, and compassion from their hearts, their eyes turn gray, hooded and lifeless.

Victimhood has one goal, no matter what form it appears to take. Its sole purpose is to teach this world is outside and apart from you. Victimhood screams "BEWARE" because there are insidious forces far stronger that have you in their snares. Yes, it proclaims "*This world of pain is real, and Truth is powerless to help you here.*" So you never probe into the deeper causes of your pain and dare not adventure inward. Since all seems fearful, miserable and chaotic on the outside, how much more terrifying must be the dark dungeons of the deep. Your victimhood never divulges how all this is a blank canvas onto which you write out your cruel intentions and superficial desires; then witness this pantomime play out before you. Once you taste your dominance and invulnerability over the world of perception, you will longer betray your conscience by preaching its victimhood.

VICTIMHOOD LEADS TO
DEFENSIVENESS

All who believe in an external world must eventually turn defensive; then strive to erect elaborate systems of protection to shield their frail bodies and weak minds! Once one invests their energies designing futile barriers, this world's outright harmlessness becomes driven out of awareness. Can a reflection attack? Nonetheless, the ego fully appreciates defensive behaviors because it knows they misdirect your energy and thought. The more extravagant and ingenious, the better because you soon forget this vast, labyrinthine maze of sophistication serves absolutely no purpose. Your defenses cannot protect you from your self-made world of fear.

There is no doubt that nursing this belief in victimhood can seem enticing, at times. It is like a magic wand we can wave in the air whenever problems and difficulties come to besiege or overwhelm us. Sometimes, it seems to offer the easiest way out of a sticky situation. So you go about brandishing the flag of your victimhood about and claim no responsibility whatsoever. However, other mind viruses soon creep into the equation, and you become mentally pervaded by notions of being defective, deficient, power-less, and impure. You begin to feel tortured by various forms of magical belief because you are reacting rather than responding to life. This activity also suppresses awareness of your divine power. Instead, you choose a plethora of potions, poisons, protections, and security devices to be your idols and saviors. It is not long before your world becomes ruled by randomness, capriciousness, madness, selfishness, cruelty and extortionary instincts. Having sucked on the luring tale of your victimhood, you throw away all hopes of Mastery. Then rapidly self-relegate into a slave of the bleak world of appearances.

THE VICTIM BANDWAGON

The victim mindset plagues the world and victims are not going out of fashion anytime soon. Victimhood manifests in many devious ways. It may appear in the form of a delinquent, a shirker, an overly indulgent being or else it can be embodied in the guise of a chronic complainer, social parasite or "innocent" pawn. Nonetheless, its essential content and taste remain the same. All victims want to push the responsibility for their screwed up lives in some other direction. After all, it is much easier to blame another for our failures than to take personal responsibility ourselves. Alternatively, we can place it squarely on the depressed socioeconomic climate, a hostile environment or a severe or totalitarian form of state power. There is no end to the justifications and rationalizations we can use as our buffer if we choose to remain a victim.

Sure, problems emerge out of nowhere, at times, that are not immediately resolvable. Life can be characterized as a tragedy in five acts. The difference is, the victim will always exploit all such dilemmas as proof of their abject powerlessness. Then they proceed to cross-pollinate their crazed notions to many domains where they could have easily exercised superior self-management, competence, and control. In the final analysis, it is none but ourselves who can be master over our thoughts, decisions, actions, and reactions. Unfortunately, many exert no mental vigilance whatsoever, and they allow their minds to fall into the gutter. So they wander about, indulging in all sorts of fantasies and wild imaginations that serve no particular purpose. Since they tune out and become unavailable to present responsibility, they function as self-paralyzed beings and can no longer function creatively towards effecting meaningful change and transformation. In the void of their self-absence, things start to go seriously downhill.

Some nurse their bitterness and resentment and others are addicted to their hostile moods and behaviors. They seem consistently ready to pounce on the tiniest incident. Hence their eyes roll incessantly from one corner to the next actively scavenging perception for the next juicy thing to attack. They become anxious and repulsed when surrounded by peace and serenity and start chattering idly or raising a ruckus to block all hopes for authentic communication. The sound of silence terrifies and overwhelms them. Some never invest even an ounce of effort in taking care of their health. Often they ravenously overeat, and avoid exercise like the plague and allow their bodies to become chemical dumping grounds for the pharmaceutical industry. The fact that they are suckers for every addiction out there does not help. Once the destined health issues appear on the horizon, they scream out in pain and then solicit sympathy for the great injustice that seems to have randomly befallen them.

Then, there are those patsies for the consumer industry who continuously overspend on an Everest of trash. Since they have no system of debt management in place, their houses readily fall into foreclosure. Many seem to gloat in their misery and parade about as victims of the system. A number are young and vitalized but are far too indolent and uppity, to ever work a job. They prefer their drug problem to the office and were booted out of their parent's home long ago. So they sleep in storefronts or the parks, and hassle every passerby for spare change, with their pit-bulls snarling beside them. They will target about half a dozen properties or cars each day to feed their voracious drug habits which often cost thousands of dollars a week. Then they mope about, giving off those snotty airs which soundlessly insinuate, that life is the one that tossed them in the ghetto. On occasion, I have come from work hoping to relax, only to find my apartment or house broken into and rampaged. One time it happened in London, and the

sixteen-year-old delinquent that cleared us out was considered by the system too young to prosecute. Another
time in Dublin, It was by a jailbird who had just escaped
from Mountjoy Prison. He was obviously very casual since
he went about tossing half-smoked cigarette butts about
while drinking a number of my beers.

A while back, I transported a friend of mine to the VA hos-
pital. There a woman quickly struck up a conversation.
Within a minute she had launched into the subtle details of
a rape she experienced twenty-six years prior while working as a cabby at night. She became overly explicit and
started delving into the lurid details, and most of what she
said, I did not want to hear. She then began jabbering
profusely about how her husband would no longer touch
her and how this event ended their marriage. Yes, the rape
had brought an end to her career, sex life and even compromised her mental health. She loved the story of her
trauma and of her innocence being violated. I suspect I was
not the first set of ears that had to hear this story out. I instinctively grasped in full panoramic splendor what an
emotional parasite and attention-grabber she had been
over the last twenty-six years. Yes, she was a psychic-
vampire soaking up all the energy waves of anyone who
would listen. In my mind's eye, I could see all the accumu-

lated carnage she had unleashed in the field of life, and it was beginning to irritate me immensely. Here tale of victimhood was too well manicured, and so I started to tune out and follow my natural thought regressions.

Sadly, she would not let the bone go. So, I decided to offload her with a question: "*What was the real reason your husband no longer touched you. Was it because he felt you invited the rape?*" She immediately answered "*Yes.*" Now the picture was coming in crystal clear. Her husband knew her intimately and was aware that she wasn't quite as innocent, as she made herself out to be. In fact, she had been going about, inviting this abuse for years before this pivotal incident occurred. That is why she took a job as a cabby and insisted on working the night shift. These were the most opportune hours. That is why she insisted on dressing provocatively, even though it was unneeded for the job. And also why he could never touch her afterward. The essential seed of infidelity was there lurking in her mind, long before the rape occurred. He had warned her not to be carrying on the way she did and about behaving flirtatiously under the neon lights. He had prognosticated such an event well in advance. The rape was inevitable; the only puzzle was why it had taken so long. And now here she was basking in all the attention, claiming victimization while sucking the lifeblood of others; from suckers like me. And she was not ashamed in the least because shame only comes to those who feel tarnished by the event, not those who consciously invite it.

Victims always proffer up a nugget or two of heartbreaking information that relates to their cruel or unfortunate plight. Just enough, to convince you they were non-complicit partners in generating their tragic circumstance. Their real intention is to portray it as a freak event that came out of nowhere that caught them wholly unguarded. They will never paint in all the colors on this canvas because then their desired image, of being seen as an "**innocent victim**" would soon be blotted out. They desire you interpret their role as that of tragic figures and passive bystanders who had no control and were non-consensual partners in the crime. The Course aims that we take personal responsibility and not search for patsies for our poor decisions. It leaves no room for compromise on this. Compromise and duplicity are languages only spoken by the ego. Perpetually hovering in a cloud of uncertainty and muddle-headed confusion, it is always ready to strike a bargain.

"I am responsible for what I see.

I choose the feelings I experience, and I

decide upon the goal I would achieve.

And everything that seems to happen to me

I ask for, and receive as I have asked."

[ACIM, T-21.II.2:3-5]

The Course proclaims that it is impossible for us to be unfairly treated in this world or for that matter in Eternity. Our Divine Will is far too strong for that! What happens is always the consequence of our arbitrary wishes and desires or else represents learning lessons we need to master. This world is swamped with the poisonous contagion of those who share the victim mindset, but we should never be tempted to consider ourselves victims. To do so is to deny our underlying divinity and teach its opposite. This foolish stance epitomizes a decision against Truth and an allegiance to the ego.

Many harsh lessons will come our way, and numerous uncalled for disasters may seem to befall us. All will tempt us to cry out our "Victim-hood" to the world. This seduction is fatal in the long run. We need to reinterpret and master our learning lessons to spiritually evolve. In this Relative World, we are always either progressing or regressing. All depends on the Voice we listen to and the decisions we make. We have no grounds for wallowing in self-pity or for entertaining crazed notions of victimization because we continuously attract all we experience. We cannot be restored to lasting peace while remaining profoundly conflicted about our Identity. While we believe, we are an effect of the world rather than its designer; we have chosen the ego. Peace only returns when we fully accept responsibility for our world.

"How else can you find joy in a joyless place except by realizing that you are not there?"

[ACIM, T-6.II.6.1:1]

Once you accept ownership, the ego will rapidly give up all pretense of friendship and turn against you. It will become overtly malicious in your moments of weakness, and many of your former friends will fade away. These were friends of your ego. They were attracted to all its pernicious ideologies and felt strengthened in this unholy alliance. They loved that senseless bantering that smacked idly from your lips, all your wild charades, malingering, hardened attitudes and deep distrust. Such was the aphrodisiac that sedated them. Your tantalizing displays of pomp and grandeur, unflinching tirades of braggadocio and endless fantasies of megalomania kept them temporarily hypnotized and spellbound to the dream. Now that show is over! Nonetheless, the first step to Mastery is embracing ownership for all your thoughts, decisions, emotions, and experiences. This is essential to regaining control over your perception and for working miracles. It will lead to your true Identity, and to everlasting safety and of peace.

The world being a mere reflection is always open to reinterpretation and here lies your path to healing. Once you think differently, you will perceive differently. If you embrace the Vision of the Holy Spirit and extend only this, you will witness a radiant realm that is timelessly fragrant and life-renewing; yet one that went unseen before. This immaculate and everlasting Reality became tarnished and submerged under the dark brush strokes of the ego. Two stories interpenetrate the canvas of your perception, but only one you will behold, in any given instant. The perception of each depends on a disparate mode of interpretation and is seen through an entirely different set of eyes. So ask whether you choose the tale of good or evil?

If you uphold only the picture of good Truth will readily reveal itself. Its gleaming unambiguous contrast to what you knew before is so extensive that the image of evil becomes entirely dispelled. So the worldly mirror disappears back inside you, and you return to awareness of your Creatorship and seamless unification with the Almighty.

DR. GOBBLERS KNOB GOES BALLISTIC

D r. Gobblers Knob was fuming again. He was exuding hostile behavior of was acting like a prize bull, once the Matador dangles the red cape before it. He felt burned up and done with life. In just a short time, he had quit his job, ended all his relationships and was moving on. Now that his fury had been finally ignited, it was rapidly gaining momentum. He kicked-off with:

"America is just one giant anthropoidal warehouse of churn and burn environments. From the jailhouses to the corporations it operates as one humongous assembly line in meat management. One craftily manipulated by the powers vested to racketeer in human ownership. All those efficiency experts and oligarchs that stand to profit from the nauseating cocktail of our sweat, blood, and brains. It seems the pigs are back in power and animal farm is open for business. I suspect it has always been so! Now we are just doing some last minute window dressing such as the building of a wall, the deportation of all Muslims and Mexicans, and our dropping out of TPP and the Paris Climate Agreement.

The only difference between the corporations and the jails is that in industry, you have to work tremendously long hours for your room and board. If you do not buy-in, you are labeled a loiterer or delinquent. The plutocracies of good old boy cronyism, which now dominate the show, make it extremely difficult for any societal outliers or fringe subcultures to survive. Have you not noticed the rapid disappearance of park benches from all our towns and villages over the past decade or so? They have all been ripped out and replaced by imposing urban sprawls and cement jungles, laced with discount stores and tacky restaurants. All perfectly designed for baiting you into buying redundant items; you will never need."

I interjected, "Surely it is not all that bad! We have one of the best highway infrastructure systems in the world and are on the cutting edge of technology. Few nations can match the beauty, majesty, and serenity of our state parks."

"That's all Hogwash!" came his swift reply. *"This country is a convoluted maze of rules, regulations, codes, statutes, and red-tape. One cannot even fart backward without requiring some clearance edict from the judiciary. There is no home-grown intelligence left because we bankrupted and decimated the educational system decades ago. It was hijacked and*

then depleted of all funds while we were still in our diapers. I think it was Nancy Reagan who first said 'No dummy left behind!' and we have been sucked down into the suffocating cesspools of protracted ignorance and mediocrity, ever since. All intelligence and expertise in imported now from the ghettoes of third world countries, all of whom will abandon us faster than a prepaid ho once the nail is banged into our coffin.

As for the state parks, they are beautiful, for sure, but try crashing in one overnight without paying for a costly pass, months or even years in advance. No! You will be awoken in the middle of the night, to find the Sheriff's muzzle pressing against your nose and a dozen flashlights in your eyes. What a buzz kill! All, peering at you like some Osama Bin Laden, while getting ready to saddle your ass with a number of felony convictions. All, priming their stun-guns so they can blast your neuroleptic centers all the way to acid Heaven. If you enjoy tempting fate, try parking your RV at the side of the road some night. Next month's mail will be a mound of overdue tickets and notices to appear. Even our beaches require paid access, and each enumerates its petty canon of unreasonable and defeatist restrictions. Because, once you subtract food, dogs, skinny dipping, diving, sex, alcohol, music, and yowling like a coyote late at night from the human equation, there is not much else to do. It just becomes one more piece of paradise, legalistically transformed into a barren entertainment wasteland, that even a nun would find impossible to endure."

"**You paint a bleak picture**," I quickly retorted! "Maybe you should just lighten up!"

"I haven't even scratched the surface!" came his quickfire response. "There is an ongoing program in place to control, subjugate and sanitize us all, by every means possible. The thought and behavior police are all around, looking to guide us down their funnels so that we drop into the buckets of acceptable behavior. Acceptable behavior, being interpreted as that which fits the norms of some vapid, soul-crushing, rigor-mortis existence. We are just like the chickens and livestock in the modern-day super-farms and slaughterhouses. Have you not noticed it at all—this silent conspiracy, I mean? Few ever see the light of day and most never get a single taste of any real freedom. Freedom is only a dream; we use to sedate the masses into abject servitude. We are all wiretapped on every click we initiate and silently being profiled for exploitation by a host of industries including healthcare, insurance, home-ownership and the like.

It will not be long before we lose rights, even over our bodies because these will become floated in certain biogenetic stocks and derivative funds. All, looking to cash-in on the projected income of our chronic sicknesses for many decades to come. All heartless enterprises that cannot afford to be out of pocket due to our untimely demise. Enforced euthanasia will be supported only for those who drop into the red letter funds. Those who require organ transplants, have costly prescriptions or need extensive healthcare or rehabilitation support will get approved. Meanwhile, our genetic predispositions and genome patterns will be stored on a giant distributed supercomputing database where it will be rigorously data-mined to determine our predispositions, susceptibilities, and overall life potential. Some will be pulverized from the get-go or sent off to work as low-level minions on the factory floors. Others will be harvested for their organs and some for their blood and bone marrow. Nanotechnology bots will be imprinted into our brain stems so that they can harness our ingenuity and creativity, even while we sleep. Our unconscious ideations will be covertly siphoned off once they reach that sweet spot, which lies just beyond the bimodal thresholds of our subliminal and supraliminal awareness."

I had enough and blurted out, "**You are one paranoid MF!**"

"If that is so, then why have the tectonic plates being gently pushing America far off into the ocean for millions of years? Yes, even Mother Nature has given us the express ultimatum to stay at least three thousand miles from everyone else. As a nation, we are like a Riker's Island of sorts, only a little bigger. There is foul and noxious scent, seeping up from our formative undergrowth and it remains a stench, impossible to eliminate or fumigate, in any conceivable way. I don't know if it's the head of Washington with his wooden teeth or all the hypocrisy we have vomited out over the last two hundred years. It is there in the Jetstream of our past aggressions and our brutal helotry of lesser territories and dominions. It has become deeply embedded in the political system, judiciary, corporations and even the mindsets of the people. We have all become servile peons, obedient automatons, and institutionalized sheep. Soon, we will be genetically barcoded and implanted with silicon devices that fully characterize our predispositions and psychological limits for rapid readout. Any notion of retaining even a modicum of personal privacy will vaporize into dust and be rapidly ridiculed as the ludicrous fantasy of a dreamy-eyed mind.

The endless massaging of stock and wealth will continue to keep the machinery of subjugation firing on all cylinders. Thus, the totem pole of our capitalistic empire will remain as a double-edged sword. The poor will be kept on their side of the financial Everest, where they will be farmed on their dreams of progress and upward mobility. They will linger as toothless outcasts, doormats and contemptible bootlickers and the elusive pot of gold; they seek will always be well beyond reach. Even the rich will be pressured to remain firmly perched on their side of the seesaw, to prevent it from losing equilibrium."

I was incensed, "You talk about this conspiracy like it is so organized and deliberate, but I cannot see any intelligent centralized hub to it all. Hell, we can't even prevent the Russkies from hacking our election process or thwart cyber-invasions on our corporate firewalls."

He continued, *"The silent manipulation of information and media instigated mind control has been in progress since Gutenberg first invented the printing press. Back then, it was used to fuel various witch-hunts, treason trials and claims of sedition. All of which led to numerous tortures, rackings, and town square impalements for the entertainment of the masses. Then, its scope was expanded to support the appe-*

tites of the power hungry. This resulted in a multiplicity of feudal scourges and Holy wars whose aim was to keep the spurious supremacy claims of the entitled class from ever been questioned or doubted. Presently, we are bombarded with grim tales of black-hooded ISIS warriors decapitating their victims, insurgent militias triggering mass genocides and Siberian Gulag Geek-boys unleashing their paralyzing cyber-spying campaigns down our classified e-conduits. We can all feel the pinch of the consumer profiling engines, phishing subcultures and identity theft circles that target and bait us so masterfully with their click traps.

Nonetheless, all is just a smokescreen, strategically designed to grab and divert widespread attention. The real treachery has always been happening behind closed doors. Now and then a new piece of toilet paper arrives on the scene upon which is scrawled in undecipherable legalese duplicitous codes and statutes which erode our rights, just a little more each day. The patriot act is just one prime example. Endowing corporations with the right to vote is another, for it entitles non-living entities the right to lobby and bribe Congress on behalf of private and exclusive interests. This transfer of power stealthily robs us all because equality is but a chimerical dream when you have no wealth. There is an insidious chilling blueprint behind this madness that suits the inter-

ests of only a few and it is purposefully contrived to make us feel all the more inconsequential in the long run. We presently live in a caste system whether you like it or not. It is just not spoken off, out loud and in the open. But just try getting your hand in in this game of high-stakes poker!

The mindless massacres at schools, cinemas, and churches will soon be ingeniously exploited as a means to remove our rights to gun ownership. It will create a massive bulwark of privacy invasion and erosion of civil liberties. Then our sheep-hood will be almost complete, and we can go, Bah! Bah! Bah! all the way to the local unemployment lines and soup kitchens! The middle-aged and spiritually broken will be ostracized and made to feel like the social equivalent of washed up courtesans making their livelihoods along the docks. Another critical aspect of this master plan of enslavement is to deprive us, of all access to real cash and resources. Shortly, all money will morph into plastic so that it can be swiftly frozen, any moment, we dare step out of line. Drones and nanotechnology bots will surveil our homes and shoulder surf our every move. All will be armed in standby mode, and ready to take us out with a blistering hail of bullets, on the click of a mouse."

I had to admit; there was some plausibility to what the Dr. was saying, even if it was heavily saturated with his usual paranoia, hyperbole and wild imaginings. I could sense this mummification process going all around me. It was like the Orwellian Nightmare was finally coming alive. America had rapidly degenerated into some unthinking Goliath that was craftily manipulated by the media. The middle class functioned more like an army of angry, belligerent Lilliputians; all jabbing with their toothpicks on the emperor's toes but powerless to pack a punch. We no longer possessed any deep-rooted values or soul. Integrity, humility, admiration, and respect had all but disappeared to make way for unruly demons, prima-donnas, emotional-ly numb addicts, and self-obsessed brats. Something smelled very rancid and dead in this dumping ground which was once alive and well. Our collective vitality, goodwill, vibrancy, and spirit of adventure had been suffocated while we were taking care of the bills. The strings, being pulled in this *Punch and Judy* show were being slyly wielded and controlled now from far beyond ourselves. How had it all happened? I had to know!

"Exactly, when was America killed—that I cannot tell you! But Fear destroyed America! Fear and wicked self-interest! The poison did not administer its lethal damage instantane-

ously. Instead, it functioned more like a slow acting deadly neurotoxin which gradually cooked our American Spirit to cinders. We all became drugged into a perpetual state of sleeplessness, characterized now by our frenzied activity, chronic anxiety, distractive behaviors and a host of new and escalating diseases. The kindest act, at present, would be to send it off, promptly, for burial with full military honors. Maybe we should give it a twenty-one gun salute. Then, we should drape a big stars and stripes flag over all 6,050,697,738 acres of it and be done with this particular experiment for good.

The beginning of our current death spiral began with the burial of Eisenhower. After that, the era of endless showmanship, smooth talking politicians and the shameless marketing of falsities began in earnest. All became immensely cosmetic, superficial, and profoundly nuanced overnight. The artificial neon lights of insincerity and dispassion turned on to light up every heart. Our heroes became those, who knew only how to flatter with shrewd and devious instant one-liners. The party was going full swing by the time JFK came to the helm. He was a crowd-pleasing poser, and an expert at promoting and disseminating short aphorisms, measured to perfection. All of a sudden, form became more important than content, and we entered a dense chiaroscuro of smoke and mirrors. Now it was all about how elegantly you spoke than what you genuinely accomplished.

Since all were held spellbound by the new media machine, it became possible to send 48,000 soldiers out to die in the killing fields of Vietnam and to justify a core deception under the umbrella of National Interest. Yes, they would have their limbs blown off, and genitalia mercilessly ripped away by bouncing betties, but all was Ok, as long as we asked them nicely and fired up their enthusiasm, at times with a dream of patriotism. To our dismay, we found self-interest could be mitigated, grievances laid aside and national guilt expunged with euphonic sounding words like '**Ask not what your country can do for you, ask what you can do for your country.**'

As this sounded perfectly reasonable, many headed off into the rice paddies to get their heads blasted away by the gooks; others preferred to be taken out in the foxholes. They may not have had their rights to vote, drink or screw yet but they were bonafide experts at being screwed through various iniquitous ideologies. Meanwhile, the commander and chief was out womanizing and playing golf, and occasionally shooting at some pheasants. He may have been completely off target, but he looked so trendy and dapper at doing it.

Soon, the movie stars, harlots, scammers and smooth talking con-artists got invited to the parade, and the age of the celebrity politician was born."

Then the genial Dr. continued, "*Did you know Skywalker was part of Color Guard at Ike's funeral? Yes, he was the only white guy invited because of his colorful personality and Oh! He looked so chic and debonair in uniform. A real son of the American people and America's sweetheart, of the male variety. Pity he ended up homeless a few years later and had to dumpster dive for his dinners. On occasion, he would stand with a cup in hand outside the local McDonalds and beg for change. So that is what a Silver Star will get ya. Perhaps, if he had realized, that he was not just burying Ike, but also America, on that day, he may have stood more to attention."*

I then inquired whether he would ever consider moving to Europe, as a more reasonable alternative.

Soon the airwaves were buzzing again with the harsh dissonant sound of his choleric rant: "*No, I wouldn't consider going there, even under the threat of death! I could never tolerate that viperous colony of super normalized beings, pompous pricks, and condescending assholes, all looking to indoctrinate you with their draconian notions about culture and etiquette. I do not have the patience to wait hours in line at some trendy restaurant on the Champs-Élysées, only to be served an exorbitantly prized morsel of undercooked horse-meat. The very thought of having to remain polite, patient and obsequious through a rumbling stomach has never been my forte. No! I would dart fast to the nearby chipper.*

It is an old-world aristocracy that aims at scrubbing you down and sweeping out all the cobwebs. All to implant certain mannerisms, social nuances and stern codes of behavior that slowly wind down your mortal coil. Soon they sap all inbuilt potential and break your spirit! Once you are properly pruned and manicured and stifled of all life, zest, color, class, and creativity they send you out to the taxidermist to implement the final touches. I see it as a maliciously crafted form of death, specifically designed for the living. It is all cleverly orchestrated by institutions so that they can feed off your carcass and milk you dry before you die. All that has ever emerged from this mold is spineless conformists laced with insufferable bourgeoisie attitudes. They spend their lives in various social dungeons surrounded by white picket fences and seek to propagate their contagion to future generations. Beware! All are supremely desiccated Methuselahs and have been exsanguinated and vitally devoured while still in their twenties. There is nothing left to say! You may as well don the butler outfit and set about polishing the silverware and sparkling the glasses. Then serve the afternoon Apéritifs to those ravenous beasts, born into fortune who will gobble it down while slyly mocking you with their sarcastic humor.

At least, in America, you get it hard and fast. You fully expect everything to be a con or deception from the get-go. You get to taste that kick in the teeth before the looney rips off your head and craps down your neck. The serial killers usually meet you with smiles before gunning you down at the local 7-11. You will have that full half second of bliss to luxuriate in before the lead from his Uzi finally enters your entrails. Maybe you will never get a chance to down that burrito, but you can thank him later for transporting you so expeditiously out of that empire of rats. For escaping the wearisome brain-drain, and harvesting of thoughts and energy."

Is there any place worth visiting?

"The pulse of life is still throbbing in the veins of many third world countries. India, South America, and Indonesia are some prime examples. They still possess some semblance of a heartbeat, but the veins of America have turned as cold and

biting as an Ice Queen long, long ago. Everything that once smelled of life got disemboweled and eviscerated and replaced with a soulless corpse. That blow-up doll of our materialistic obsessions is filled now only with the hot air of self-serving politicians and money manipulators. At least we have our laughing gas at the cost of thirteen trillion. Our sterile calculating culture is about as friendly and inviting as the surface of the moon. All that remains is the hallowed ground of the Civil War battlefields, but unfortunately, all the spilled blood can never be invigorated back to life.

This barren and plastic culture is incapable of orgasm because it no longer functions as a living organism. It has to take Viagra and a host of other drugs just to get it up. Meanwhile, it jockeys around the world behaving like some schoolyard bully making wild claims about its potency. In truth, this sweaty cauldron of mongrels and hybridized half-breeds, they call a melting pot has no redeeming values. Any residual altruism it ever enjoyed, has long been replaced by all-out greed without any bounds or limit. Any modicum of free thinking, speech or action it once enjoyed has long been replaced with social subjugation. The plenum of our former potentiality got converted into a funeral pyre onto which we heaped our gods of innovation, inspiration, benevolence, and justice. Now, our cruel disciplinarian parent enjoys callously *brandishing her whip about and mindlessly lacerating her children. Nonetheless, it was we the sheeple who witlessly invited her to the throne. The artistic and visionary were the first victims, the first to meet with her blood-drenched pincers and the first to be nudged off the edge of the chessboard into the infinite abyss of chronic poverty and social alienation. For her royal aim has always been to dehumanize all truly gifted minds before abandoning them to the gulags of our inner-city ghettoes and sewers.*

All hippies, beatniks and iconoclastic dissidents became rapidly frozen out, in this New World Order, so that we could preserve our frenzied isolationist culture of scurrying ants. For we seek only to nourish the strait-laced conformist and lip zipped and have no place now for heathenish bohemians like Kerouac, Miller, and Ginsburg. No!, you will find all such social outliers up in the attic next to the mannequins. Do not be put off by their emaciated looks and torn out eyes for all such fringe groups have long degenerated into the admirable psychopaths and serial killers we have always deserved. They were always destined to melt like Swiss cheese, and drip through the pores of their autogenous insanities. Do not be too dismayed either by the robotic movements and glass-eyed appearances of our herd mentality for all such factory bootlickers go about having terrifying nightmares in their sleep of falling down the chasms and cracks in our social matrix. It is a little sad that all genuineness and authenticity became substituted by the thin veneer of superficiality, while respect and comradeship took a brutal trampling. But the masters and experts of our Military-Industrial complex need to make their quotas and thus beat all humanity out of us with the muzzle of their guns.

Ask what great gem has crystallized from the immense force and intense heat of our pressure cooker environments? What has bubbled up as a consequence of our chronic stress, distress, heartache, and mental diarrhea? All I detect is the many-headed hydra of corporate authoritarianism together with its intolerance and pointless displays of power as it double deals its way around the world searching for yet another tax shelter to hide in. It is truly an ugly beast, and one painted with so many devious faces and phony smiles. I see the frightening visages of its self-righteousness, superiority, specialness, mercilessness, emptiness, and insatiable rage as well as hypocrisy, cunning, and duplicitous schemes of legerdemain. What remains is a veritable cauldron of the half-living and half-dead. Thoroughly broken spirits and uncultivated barbarians with zealous eyes and filthy lips. I think it would be better to head back to our Flint mobiles and charter a return journey into the Neolithic or Pleistocene eras.

That would be far more fruitful and illuminating than trying to exhume the carcass; we have now. Maybe we should slip back on our tails and enter the primordial soup of the subaqueous realms, rather than press that dial for future."

So Dr. Gobblers Knob had finally flipped! It was to be expected, after all, since his immense hate and cynicism, knew no limits. He had always been simmering to the boil, and now most certainly had entered a meltdown and psychological implosion of massive proportions. He had finally transformed into that admirable monster of pure savagery, and cold-blooded contempt, that he was always destined to become. I too knew that freedom, at the political and social levels, has always been a myth and that countries like China and North Korea were brutal and lethally repressive cultures, full of indoctrination, tyrannical oppression and rigorous censorship. Dare to speak up about anything at all, and you will fast find lead in the back of your head. Even the more moderate regimes had serious issues to contend with. There was to be no freedom for the masses! That was always an illusion! However, an individual could decide not to buy in and gain personal Mastery through their own efforts and dedication.

Once attained, that outer culture or authority would be powerless to subdue him. Even were it to place him in chains, or torture and whip him about in the public square, he could still smile. Jesus was one prime example of such a Master. He continued to teach Love and Healing in the face of cruel and bloodthirsty influences and interests. Abandonment, ridicule, brutality and even crucifixion could do nothing to break the power of his will, and he continues to shine as a beacon of light and compassion to all who tune in to this day. Assuredly, the only freedom, ever to be found is in one's mind and thought, and unless you attain mastery there, you will always be a slave. You must succeed in slaying your ego, or freedom will remain just a pipe dream.

This half-crazed culture, you see now is nothing but the outer face of our inner emptiness. Behind the faceplate of our numerous masks lies the ego at the control booth projecting it uncaring attitude, selfishness and preferred boundaries to all. This is the real reason, we are miserable most of the time, and why we entertain no trust, cower in fear and lock all our doors. We banish most to the wastelands of our mind where they remain in a perennial disenfranchised discombobulated state. They become to us an Antediluvian species or Cro-magnon herd of misfits that we would like to outsource and farm in the cracks of Uranus's ass. We quickly disparage all who are not a perfect photocopy of our vile calculating thought because we fear being overwhelmed by what could genuinely transform us. Eternal existence remains seamlessly unified, but the sinister offspring of the ego makes the One appear as many. Our ancient cry of victimization has always been a deceitful ruse designed to fool only suckers, nitwits simpletons. In truth, we remain victims only of ourselves. It is we alone who choose our slavery, yet we can also choose to emancipate ourselves.

Our deep-seated resentfulness and never-ending litany of grievances evidence nothing more than our essential meanness, villainy, and lack of celebration in the joys of "others." Our fathomless hate is the natural consequence of our choice for ego empowerment. Yet, it is we alone who give it free reign, as our Master and Commander. All that goes on in our control booths, 24x7, is Projection! Projection! Projection! Thus we remain severely dissociated and profoundly sick. Our little white lies and economies of truth cannot save us. Unless we become well-intentioned, authentic, compassionate beings, we will never reach our deepest core and heal. Sadly, this is a voyage we dare not take, and so we remain bound to this tragicomedy, without end. All we can do is hover about in the fear clouds quipping out our sly little jokes and vengeful humor while ravenously exploiting comedy, to vomit out our uncontainable prejudice and hate. Yes, there is much that is loathsome and nefarious that seeps through the pores of our seemingly innocuous opinions. Our true intention has always been to stick blades into the backs of all.

DISSOCIATION AND PROJECTION

Nothing exists without a cause, and nothing survives without some source of fuel. Our bodies, for example, need food, exercise and sleep to endure. Likewise, our minds require meaning and purpose, or we soon develop various forms of mental sickness and spiritually fade. The ego and the Relative World cannot perpetuate on their own. The twin dynamics of **(1) Projection** and **(2) Dissociation** are the crown jewels of its entire survival campaign. These alone seem to certify it with the illusion of existence. Projection leads to dissociation and dissociation, in turn, pictures the distortionary universe of endless mayhem that keeps the fire going. Only those who believe in separation bother to project while those who have recognized underlying unity take full responsibility for what they perceive and experience. No one attacks their reflection in the mirror unless they are decidedly insane.

The diagram depicts the causal link between denial and fear. Denial does not lead directly to fear unless there is first projection. Projection, in turn, leads to the severely dissociated state of split-mind from which fear derives all the nourishment it requires to propagate and flourish.

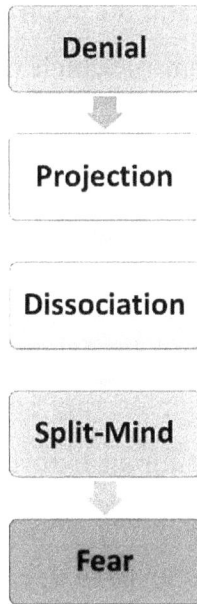

THE CAUSAL LINK FROM DENIAL TO FEAR

All our problems began with our denial of our Creator. Our *Tiny Mad Idea* (TMI) was the pestilential seed that appeared to drive us out of Heaven. Since then, its deleterious effects have expanded, transmogrified and proliferated to the point where we now have become strangers, even to ourselves. Denial of our true Identity led to projection and condemnation. Even so, we only condemn others for what we first condemned in ourselves. We interpreted certain repressive "dark" thoughts and behaviors as utterly contemptible and enshrined them into irrevocable sins. So we placed ourselves beyond all hope of redemption. The fundamental belief system to which we now align covers our original denial and self-deception and it enables our mad belief in sin to thrive unhindered.

For example, those who hold entrenched beliefs in their physical existence tend to deemphasize and dismiss the spiritual domain. Their earthly self-conception will be of some carcass, inhabiting an exterior world rather than as of the spiritual powerhouse that is continuously fabricating the world of their experience. Their sole interest will be in immersing themselves more in the world of their experience as opposed to comprehending how their underlying thought processes shape and project it. Likewise, they will perceive all boundaries, partitions, and separations as real, and fail to see these as a mind-generated mesh carved out of their judgments and beliefs.

It must be evident that our apparent state of dissociation produces fear and that fear is impossible where there is no dissociation. The only astute and insightful question then is in asking whether our dissociated state is real or just a hoax? That is! Do all false and deceptive appearances; we perceive merely reflect apparitions produced by our dissociated mind-state or are they inescapable hardwired realities? As long as we believe in such appearances, our minds remain split and our false identity is secured. It is from this false self-concept that all illusions snowball. Since we will continue to deny aspects of our Whole Self, the consequence is extreme confusion, spiritual darkness, and seemingly irresolvable contradictions. These "external" aspects soon become the landfills towards which we steer all garbage trucks of our thought. We no longer take responsibility for our world but project culpability instead for all the madness and misfortune to the "outside" world. Naturally, the secret vault of our most treasured sins, petty hates, and wicked condemnations will become projected to all.

Our salvation then can only be in extracting all the pleasure and notoriety, we can get from life, before finally kicking the bucket. And we will direct all our attention and energy towards keeping the halo of our specialness and uniqueness, alive and glowing. We will listen attentively whenever the ego entices us with some alluring fantasy of our freedom and independence. Doing so, we will never realize, how our dream of self-autonomy is nothing but a guaranteed path into increased bondage. One, in which we voyage deeper into the dark kingdoms of illusion. A separated body enjoys no real freedom because it is not real. Freedom is only ever to be had through recognizing our unassailable unity with all. This intimate connection is what guarantees our Eternal protection, invulnerability, and strength. It transports us to the very Source of our Sovereign Power. When we abandon all ego temptations and heed the worthless no longer, and listen not to endless cries of victimhood, our true Reality becomes inescapable and pellucid.

THE EGO'S SEDUCTIONS

L et's speak plainly, for a moment. We all have the firm conviction that we can continue to enjoy health, happiness, peace, and abundance while others remain sick, miserable, conflicted, and deprived. We are supremely confident that we can make rapid progress while others collapse, go bankrupt and speedily deteriorate. We do not truly believe their perpetual state of anxiety, unnecessary hardship and failure to actualize their potential can have any bearing on our lives. Such is the ego dream of success, but it can only last for a while. No ego genuinely interprets the paths of collaboration and self-interest as the same. Nor can it comprehend how the lamentable wails of others portend its impending future misery. It cannot cognize how these thorns it perceives everywhere are omens that forewarn its inevitable doom.

All this, ego nonsense, undeniably goes against the **Law of Mind,** which succinctly states that **what we believe is possible for others must eventually come for us**. This reflexive action on the part of existence is unavoidable because *the outside* is nothing but a mirror reflecting our inner thoughts. The shrine of perception faithfully depicts nothing but our intentions. If our intentions are cruel, we will perceive a world of cruelty. When we believe we can take, we will surely lose, and once we place our faith in the power of sickness, it will promptly come knocking on our door. The many demons we perceive, are the frightening visages of our subjective ideations. They become enlivened to the screen of perception through the projection of our thought. So long as we fail to forgive our world, we will never reintegrate and heal.

The specialness we seek will surely kill. Nonetheless, this is the crown jewel of all ego seductions, and it leads directly into our chronic states of dissociation and perpetual conflict. Specialness makes contrasts of every conceivable variety so that it can maintain its sandcastles of illusion. Someone must be driven to the gutter so that another can rise into a God. One must be seen as inferior, to advance the myth of our individual superiority. Our specialness cunningly exploits judgment to produce its lineup of the unworthy ones. Sins, weaknesses, and deficiencies must be seen everywhere, except in ourselves. It is this that preserves the veneer of our innocence, virtue, and perfection. The aureole of our illusory innocence constantly feeds off fresh meat and so it must sentence and condemn all as aggressors when it becomes opportune. Yes, they are the guilty party, your honor!

What does this callous and misdirected approach generate but a world of savageness, cruelty, and fear! Our mean-spirited demands call for endless wars and vicious cycles of violence and abuse. Our wish to extract ruthlessly at any cost produces a world of scarcity, that is rampant with famines and loss. Our inner vulnerability, once projected, fashions a bleak landscape of sickness and death. Every aspect and shred of our perception is the spontaneous by-product of some belief, that became projected. The only escape from this vortex of madness and misery is in recognizing *"There is no world apart from my idle wishes; all is the unavoidable outcome of my ego investments."* Fear will continue to escalate until you make no more demands. Only when you become neutral and impartial will the light-filled Kingdom emerge back into view.

THE COLLECTIVE PROJECTION OF FEAR

Anyone can see that those countries who stockpile armaments, nuclear weapons, chemical agents, etc. are often very fearful and repressive ones. North Korea is an obvious example. Such nations seek to isolate themselves from the rest of the world, and they fervently hoard and accumulate all available wealth and resources. They like to consider their hostile takeovers, as Holy Wars or campaigns of harmonization and repatriation. Such was the catch cry of Russia in its recent annexation of Crimea. Justifications and euphemisms abound such as relabeling a hostile attack as a strategic defense. Other colorful euphemisms include referring to missiles and ICBMs as *protectors*, and *peacemakers*, rather than *intimidators*. Notice how our governments like to nickname weapons of mass destruction with quaint names like *little boy*. The intention is obvious, to anyone not already blinded by the seductions of patriotism and power. But many are extremely vulnerable to pernicious ideologies lurking just below the surface.

The same dynamic plays out among various groups, sects, and races. Claims to racial purity enable thoughts of impurity to be projected to other races. All of which progresses the dehumanization of inferiors, who are then rapidly seen, as infidels or poisoners of the well. Apart from the malicious brutalities and atrocities that follow, there are often systematic and cold-hearted crusades to support genocide, segregation, extermination, and decimation. Specific eugenic initiatives may be enforced to weed out the chaff from the grain, to bar any chance of it stomping its feculent imprint on the genetic future. So the ancient beast roams about proudly showing its horns. Earlier last century, we saw this beast prowling in Armenia, Greece, the Soviet Union and Nanking. Then it hit the road and clicked its heels together to join the Third Reich. Not long after that, it sauntered onward, to support numerous genocides in Indonesia, Ethiopia, Cambodia, and Burundi. In recent years, we have seen its face again with all the horrors that have unfolded in Iraq, Yugoslavia, Rwanda, and Sudan. The motivating agents and forces are almost always the same, as are the mechanics, methods, and outcome.

But are we brave enough to observe the dynamic of projection, a little closer to home? Can we look nakedly at our self-generated projections and own them. See the fear, guilt, and inadequacies we so willingly project to others while remaining in stark denial of its source within ourselves? We all have our little treasure chests of vanities that we dare never mention. It can be anything from our physical appearance, innovative ability, business acumen, athletic prowess or even sense of humor. Just about anything can be used as a source of vanity.

When I was an Engineering undergrad, I was always broke and in perpetual need of additional income. Inwardly, I was proud of my mathematical abilities and was already solving advanced calculus problems, at sixteen. So I started giving tuition to local students living in the area. Thus it was that I found myself cruising up on my motorbike, one day, to a rather modest and unassuming home. I was feeling on top of myself, as I took my sunglasses off and entered this humble abode. The father was a blue collar worker of lower middle class, and he worked for some local construction outfit. Naturally, the mother wanted the best education possible for her son. I guess her greatest fear was that he would be caught in the same mousetrap, as his dad. She pressed me to give him tuition on Maths and Applied Maths and seemed ready to pay any amount, I wished.

I agreed and fired off the first session with some calculus questions which I had found tricky. It soon became apparent that he knew the entire field. I was also extremely dismayed by how rapidly he worked them out. When the session came to an end, I took the money and quickly left. The following week, I came a little more meekly to the door. I decided to knock the wind out of his sails by picking one of the most challenging problems I knew, in matrix theory. Soon, I found myself silently imploding within since he answered it with ease. What to do now? What could I teach? And there he was just looking blankly at me with a face so innocent and trusting. He was so grateful to have me there because he had finally someone to whom he could relate. Someone, who could recognize the grave plight, he was in. He was, enacting the drama of the gifted child before me, and peering out through those beautiful eyes, which were so calm, serene and powerful. It all felt like some cruel joke. Like being caught on the wrong end of *Good Will Hunting.*

For a while, it was so entrancing and mesmerizing, being baked in that sun. Feeling hypnotized and bodiless with the partitions all gone. We were no longer frightened ghosts haunting the specter of humanity but divine presences communicating at a level far higher than words. Yes, words had suddenly become the rankest superfluities; no proxies were needed for us to communicate fluidly, and from a far more elevated, abstracted and heavenly domain. Instantly, I realized that I had never really known true communication before and what a sublime experience it was. The game of masks and superficialities, defenses and power plays had always functioned as an intrusive barrier, in the past. Everybody had been a beggar, until this moment. There to take advantage of me, or to have their feathers stroked. Never before and never since have I met someone with whom I could communicate so purely and effectively. I await still, and now a quarter of a century has dripped down the well. That day, I became the sheep who had unwittingly stepped into the wolf's lair, and it was profusely clear to me who was on the menu for lunch. I needed to get away from it all. Who fucks with perfection! The whole situation seemed to tarnish my integrity; in short, it made me feel like a fraud. So, I ended it abruptly and never came back!

Eventually, I came to see the situation, for what it was. His parents had been projecting their inadequacies and insecurities to their son while remaining blind to his real genius. Sadly, many are drowning fast in the pool of mediocrity, due to the projection of our inherent limitations and sour begrudging attitudes. So some find their remarkable insights, ingenuity, talents and progressive approaches continuously go unheard. They are being trampled on and annihilated by the hoof of the pigs. Society holds many lives captive because it shuns and abhors all exalted abilities, that it cannot fathom or comprehend. The best of us are ostracized, rather than celebrated, isolated rather than embraced. Moored on particular ice-packs and frozen out from humanity; then silently left to float off into the Bering Straits.

Miss PTSD

I had this friend for many years, who was a rare soul. She was someone, with the capacity to trigger immense changes in my perspective, even on our first meeting. She was a very bubbly figure and possessed an uncanny intuition, and she was always finely tuned to the greater picture. Being nobody's fool, she penetrated directly to the heart of any matter and often would predict improbable events, well in advance. Sometimes, she would shudder or vent her annoyance, on prognosticating some catastrophic event that was just up ahead. Often she would detect some pernicious evil; all had overlooked. Nevertheless, the entire landscape of her deeper psychology seemed completely frozen in time, and she retained the emotional maturity of a young girl. This disconnect between her intellectual and emotional maturity, I found most fascinating, if not disarming. She remained a mystery which I never expected to unravel. When our friendship strengthened, she began to flesh out some of her life experiences. It was evident that her dominant obsession was with her childhood and early adolescence. She began describing how her brother was hit by a drunk driver while they were out playing in the snow. He was only seven years old at the time, and she was nine. Because of the critical and life-changing injuries, he endured, he had the greatest difficulties accomplishing simple things like walking, talking and eating. He had only the use of one arm, and on this, he could only maneuver two fingers with any proficiency. Over time, he had developed a massive hunchback and had to walk in a crouched manner. He most certainly resembled a Quasimodo of the modern era. When I would see him walking about in the snow, I would instantly get internally flooded with scenes from the movie, *Ethan Frome*.

Since she lived on the other side of the states, I only visited her on a few occasions. When I would come to visit, she would concede to let me take him out with us to eat at a public restaurant. She was extremely embarrassed, if not mortified, by his presence in a social context because when he ate, food would spew, dribble and ooze out from the sides of his mouth and splatter in all directions. He made such a mess that other patrons would quickly move away. She related, how on some occasions, they had been asked to leave. Normally, I am beyond embarrassment, but even I was beginning to cringe. Here he was mirroring some great amorphous blob of blubber, surrounding this vortex of organic suction power through which he was shoveling it in. Now and then, some random emissions would emanate

from his maw, as lava spurts out from the mouth of Kilau-
ea.

He was in his late fifties but very positive and dauntless in
his attitude and about to complete his Master's degree. I
could only imagine how incredibly difficult; it must have
been for him; since he could only type with one finger in a
weird Woody Woodpecker style. Major phases of my natural life would pass while I witnessed him typing just a single sentence. Now after six years, he was almost complete.
One had to admire his passion and endurance, and all I
could think of was *Shawshank Redemption*. Yes, I was having flashbacks of that movie and in particular that scene,
when the lead actor, Andrew Dufresne finally describes the
key ingredients to his breakout as being the work of pressure and time.

Anyway, here he was relaxed, calm, and confident in demeanor. His sense of humor was intoxicating, and he had
long put away all the tragedy and sorrows from his youth.
Never once, did I detect even the tiniest trace of self-pity or
a cry of victimhood. As time went on, I learned how their
parents had blamed his sister entirely for his accident. She
should have been watching over him more closely, they
said. She was the patsy, who was made to feel overwhelm-

ingly guilty for ruining his life while growing up. This one event was continually used a whipping stick to beat her down. So this was how the games of psychological warfare proceeded in their particular slice of domestic paradise! She was endlessly harassed and emotionally / psychologically tortured beyond measure in her formative years. She never went into the finer details, since she felt thoroughly ashamed of the event and sadly had bought in, to some of the guilt and blame projected in her direction. They made her feel so undeserving of the health she enjoyed while her brother suffered and even unworthy to be alive. This continuous persecution exercised a tremendous influence in shaping her psyche. To add insult to injury, she was mocked, and ridiculed incessantly by many kids, at the local school on account of her brother's pitiful and laughable demeanor.

Being naturally friendly and open-minded, she would often swim in the same pool, as the black kids while her mother was at work. One day, however, her mother swung by unexpectedly and witnessed this for herself. She savagely grabbed her by the arm, took her home and pushed her up against a full-length mirror. Then started taunting her by saying "*Look at yourself, you are turning black.*"

All her teenage dreams and girlish aspirations had become fatally crushed and annihilated because of that one moment of recklessness, on behalf of the drunk driver. So, one day, I asked her, "*Where were your parents at the time of the accident?*" She responded, informing me, that they were never at home and always too busy with their personal lives. They let the kids take care of themselves. Nonetheless, the extent of psychological pain inflicted was truly immense, even to me who was witnessing it many decades later. I began to smell a rat in the cruel way her parents had treated her. They undoubtedly had used her as a guinea pig to alleviate their personal feelings of guilt. They made her into the target instead to wash from their consciousness their contribution to the tragedy by letting her alone to take care of her brother.

As a consequence, she became emotionally traumatized and numb from the moment of the accident and could never emotionally mature. The period before that tragic event was her safety zone. That which came afterward was full of uncertainty, pain, anxiety, torment, ridicule, guilt and an intense fear of freak events. It became an instant of existential discontinuity that she could never emotionally navigate past. She could never leap across that gap of terror. Maybe if her parents had shown her more love and understanding instead of showering her with their guilt and blame, she might have overcome the trauma and found some solace and strength. Perhaps, over time, she may have gained self-esteem, confidence and a firm conviction in her value. However, the damage had riveted into the far reaches of her psyche, and it left permanent scars that would never heal. That is why I refer to her, as Miss PTSD.

The ego propaganda machine never stops. It wants to convince us that we can escape what we dump onto others. Such is its entire strategy for cleaning house and attaining peace of mind. It never highlights the intrinsic cost or damage, to ourselves, arising from our indiscriminate use of projection. It is indisputable, however, that we can never escape the prison-house of our innermost thoughts and beliefs. Whenever we project, we are choosing to remain unhealed, chronically disempowered and severely dissociated. Our perceptions then run dark from what we attempt to shovel onto others.

The secret vaults of our mind and the display case of our thoughts, we are powerless to escape. We are haunted by our intentions if they be malicious and unjust. All of which can make us feel engulfed in the horrifying spectacle of our projections. Life is quite a burlesque showpiece, and it presents to our senses a very intimidating crew of motley fig-ures that rattle and bedevil us. They will remain to terrify until we recognize their actions and behaviors are molded from within. These stark chimerical appearances are fash-ioned entirely from the fury and vengeance, we continu-ously project. Projection tears out our eyes and robs us of vision. It invites fear, to be our only companion. Our an-guish and trepidation can intensify to such an extreme that we willingly self-isolate and go berserk.

You may well Ask, "*How can I heal my severe state of disso-ciation and reach Salvation?*" The Course provides the an-swer. It teaches the opposite of projection is extension, and the opposite of dissociation is unification/integration. "**Extension**" is the cure-all dynamic for relinquishing all hideous miscreations born from our use of projection. Once these mentally generated phantasms disappear, we begin to perceive the Real World. This constitutes a light-filled haven in which we are immersed in bliss. In this meaningful, potent and creative paradise, we come to rec-ognize our unity with our "brothers," and are healed of our dissociated condition.

Projection propagates the ego's wrong-mindedness and increases the belief in separation. Extension, on the other hand, can be powerfully deployed to reinforce right-understanding and to unify. The dynamic of extension embodies holding right intentions and teaching this in our actions and behaviors. So we come to heal as opposed to harm and to empower rather than to exploit. As we genuinely listen we feel safe to drop our defenses and to abandon our instruments of manipulation and control. Having liberated ourselves, we can free others. As integration increases, we become truly healed, and spiritual light floods the screen of our perception. Then the happy dream begins in earnest and the unfading light of the eternal starts showing up around familiar objects and people. Slowly it suffuses its benevolence and spiritual magic across the entire canvas, and encompasses all, in its soft embrace.

Meanwhile, it soon becomes evident that these "others" are not bodies but integral aspects of our original Identity. They are pivotal to our healing because we all share in the greater Reality of Unity. From diving deep within, we discern the wisdom of forgiving all apparent transgressions in the world around us. All actions, events, and situation do not occur at random but follow directly from our learning needs. Interpreted sagaciously, they will be seen as a blessing. Sadly, our ego interprets and deciphers all events under a poor light, and so it coerces us into decisions that go against our best interests.

There are immutable spiritual laws that can help us differentiate the false and insubstantial from the limitlessly valuable. Learning the correct criteria for evaluating decisions and for distinguishing the worthy from the worthless will help relinquish all impediments to Truth. Once we bring a halt to the ego's engines of projection and madness, we become happy and healed. Then our apparent dissociated state is no more. It has always been a consequence of our endorsement of error which imposes a mental overlay over our Spiritual Reality. Likewise, it induces our fallacious experience of operating through a split-mind. Once we rid all error from our thought, we will enter the Kingdom in full awareness.

IDOLS, ECLIPSING OUR SPIRITUAL VISION

A mind in pain will clutch at any straw. Seeing itself surrounded by a sea of meaninglessness and futility, it becomes extremely vulnerable to the attraction of idols. In our fear-weakened state, idols can seduce and hypnotize us completely. The relative world comprises a veritable panorama of deities, icons, and temptations; all exhibited in such alluring forms. Their diversity ranges from the physical and psychological to the spiritual. They are the ego's replacement for Heaven, and the chief temptation it pitches to those who wish to dream. Sadly all idols must inevitably fail because they are not part of the fabric of Reality. The ego's entire plan of salvation hinges on selling you numerous enticing dreams in the external world, hoping you will treasure these in place of eternal Truth. In some dreams, you are a hero or conqueror while in others you wallow in sensual indulgence or become a willing surrogate or slave. Some of these dreams aim to bestow the specialness and prestige that God denied you while others preach your frailty and victimhood before your Creator. Religion is a particularly insidious form of idol worship, that attracts through selling the concept of an afterlife. It spellbinds by offering the prospect of a golden future; you just need to make some small sacrifices now. It never informs that the true cause of your continued misery is your spiritual ignorance. In contrast, enlightened wisdom reminds that only in the present can your conflicted state ever be resolved. Unfortunately, instead of living wholly, fearlessly, and conscientiously NOW and entering the Eternal Paradise, we temporally project our hopes of salvation to the future.

The mundane mind focuses on making future investments rather than executing its present power. This is the prevailing attitude the world over. We are pressured by idiots to engage means that accomplish nothing. Taught that if only we recite enough rosaries, do enough penances and flog our backs until they are raw, all will be ok. All ceremonies, processions, confessions, sacrifices, deprivations, and acts of self-torturing are of no worth. They merely reflect the ego's delight in indulging in an ostentatious show of pomp, glory, and sacrifice. Such practices obfuscate the natural light of spirit and imbue each with the belief that pain and suffering are the truth. Apparently, this how the ego thinks but it is hardly how God's Mind does. The esoteric meaning of the scriptures becomes lost to those under the spell of this delusion. All who subscribe to it believe their real nature is sinful. Their conviction is that sinfulness is sacred and impregnable and that it can only be atoned for through trivial pursuits and rituals. Nonetheless, all forms of penance impute a malicious and vengeful intent to God. Mindless repetition and self-flagellation assert that God is wrong in His Creation and that Heaven needs to be bought through mellifluous, euphonic sounding words and senseless acts.

The present moment is complete and powerful enough to vaporize all your foolish fantasies, doubts and misunderstandings, in an instant. It is not just the golden **GatewayToEternity**; It contains Eternity in its entirety because Eternity does not spread itself across time. Time is an illusion and can therefore never have a meeting place with Truth. Those who are willing to live purely and expansively in the present will be without fear. Such Enlightened Beings entertain no fantasies concerning the afterlife because they are already experiencing Heaven in the *Here-and-Now*. Their indestructibility, God's glory and the utter dependability of His unfailing Love is self-evident to them every moment. Religion, as it exoterically practiced, is nothing more than a thinly disguised form of spiritual materialism. Instead of heaping up sacks of physical or psychological rewards and merits in the present, one is accumulating them for the afterlife. However, unless your primary thought is transformed and purified, at a fundamental and foundational level, nothing at all will have been accomplished. Your world will remain the same humdrum, fear-based existence that will follow your thoughts everywhere you go. Eventually, it will dawn that you have always been traveling inside yourself.

The idols of materialism, physical pleasure, comfort and worldly security, we all are very familiar with since they are undisguised and out in the open. We find them easier to relate to and more comprehensible to digest because most believe they are bodies. Since specialness is a subtle psychological idol, we find far harder to discern and expunge. Fame, accomplishment, glory, notoriety, recognition, worldly power, flattery, adoration, supplication and so much more must be included under the banner of specialness. The ego dreams of attaining specialness by all means possible. Specialness is the elusive trophy towards which it steers the ships of men to their inevitable doom. The vainglorious pursuit of specialness can be allegorically compared to Custer's Last Stand since it represents the last holdout of the ego.

THE BARRIER OF GRIEVANCES

Grievances do not arise in isolation but are the inevitable outcome of idol worship and dream attachment. Grievances are like the inevitable vapor stream trailing behind the supersonic jet of your idols. They become more pronounced whenever any of your relative world fantasies are threatened. Choosing the transient and worthless they proliferate because conditions always change. Once the mirage that supports your chosen idol evaporates, grievances promptly appear. Meanwhile, the ego is down in the boiler room, getting ready to add more fuel to the fire. Any moment one of your pet desires or prospects is imperiled, it jumps up and is pissed. Suddenly you find your mind flooded with grievances and you experience intense feelings of victimization from a cruel and savage world. Somehow, this broken down, unstable existence does not love you enough since it is unwilling to appease your whimsical aspirations or lusts. At a deeper level, grievances reflect your profound conviction that God's Love is not sufficiently bountiful because He failed to meet your specialness demands. Beliefs in scarcity and incompletion are perpetually reinforced in the presence of grievances.

As you thread your way through your day, your mind is bubbling with hundreds, if not thousands of grievances. At any given moment, you are only consciously aware of a few. The remainder slip into the background to run as silent, unconscious processes on the server farm of your ego. These processes await the opportune moment when they can rise to hijack your thought. Though subconsciously lurking, grievances nonetheless shape and influence your entire worldview. They establish your moods, adjust your attitudes and determine what types of activities and behaviors you will likely engage. By modifying and programming the filters of your thought, they predetermine what risks and adventures you will undertake, and what sort of experiences and friends you will attract. They set the entire tone of your personality.

For example, suppose that your chosen idol is wealth and security. This idol will compel you to be grievance orientated whenever there are rising costs, stock market fluctuations, new taxes, any material upsets, etc. It will paralyze your capacity to fully live because you will interpret your time as equivalent to money. Likewise, it will sabotage your relationships because you will be disinclined to squander "idle" time with your wife and children. In contrast, you will use your time and energy exclusively to further your wealth accumulation goals. Thus seduced by this idol you narrowband and limit the greater dimensions of your life.

Maybe you don't give a hoot about money but admire intelligence, ingenuity, and wit. This idol will incline you to be intolerant of the less gifted. The dullards of the world will repulse, annoy and inflame you tremendously. The moment they begin to say anything lame, redundant or moronic, your blood will boil over. You will often quickly retaliate by attacking and condemning them for their glaring inferiority. You may even conclude that they should not be allowed to live and consume planetary resources. The entire antenna of your focus will be fervidly directed towards analyzing and scrutinizing the pervasive ignorance and ills of society, enumerating the problems of government and cutting the legs out from under another. You will fume and explode into fits of vitriolic ranting and engage in tirades of frenzied madness over the tiniest matters. All are unworthy of your superior presence because this form of specialness is your chosen god and idol. Your aristocratic ears will never listen to the uncultivated greenhorns in your midst or anyone else hailing from the antediluvian era.

Most are completely unaware of the real cost of their grievances. Not only do grievances serve to alienate you from others, but the deep-seated hostility and turmoil they foster, make real peace impossible. All sublime, elevated and loving thoughts become barred from conscious access. Only to be mercilessly trampled upon like freshly blossoming flowers by the toxic spring of your grievances. Thus you live out your entire life in the mythical private kingdom of your self-sanctioned superiority. Grievances bind your mind to the past and obfuscate all hopes of vision in the present. Idols, in contrast, charter you on a course into an imaginary future; and one guaranteed to disappoint.

Temporally, their direction may be different, but in function and content, they remain the same. Both share the purpose of entangling you further in the minefields of time and illusion. Consequently, your awareness gets channeled and directed towards chasing the shadows of the worthless and quixotic. The eternal light of spirit becomes powerless to penetrate past the dark nebulous clouds your grievances continuously circulate and suffuse over all aspects of your perception. Thus, the fountainhead of miracles within which could liberate is temporarily held on check and Truth becomes sacrificed on your altar of idol worship. All this is only a tiny part of the immense cost.

Regrettably, you are only too glad to pay because each idol attracts through some exceptionally seductive temptation. Each preaches to your willing and sympathetic ears that it alone has the power to make you whole; and that it will succeed where all the rest have failed. So you bite into the chocolate covered poison and are soon drugged into a state of deep sleep. You will not awaken until you become despairing enough to sacrifice all idols.

THE TRUE INGREDIENTS OF IDOL WORSHIP

Misery creates a powerful, circumferential force-field around itself, akin to that of antimatter. Inside this force-field, idol worship gains great appeal. Those who are content have no need for idols, but deeply tormented souls, lost in the gray world of chronic boredom, mediocrity, hopelessness, debt, unremitting suffering, and persistent overwork will seek some earthly compensations. Various fantasy lands must be ideated upon and then projected onto the screen of the void. Enticing dreams must be flushed down their neural pipe-ways to cover this drab world over. If we can not taste the paradisiacal bliss directly, we can at least experience it vicariously through entertaining a mixed bag of spellbinding holographic simulations. Our banal existence must provide something for us to latch onto, or we will string ourselves up and set the mannequin a' rocking.

Idols come to the rescue wherever there is a bleak picture. They are mirages in time that aim to fill the cup of our never-ending despondency. To join the ego's club, each must expeditiously amass a portfolio of worthy idols. Naturally, the ego deems the present insignificant and overlooks it entirely. It charters you, instead, on a breathtaking voyage into the future. It asserts that a little up ahead your dream-house, financial security, and some nice piece of tail await you and a measure of blow thrown into the bargain, All you have to do is commit yourself to digging ditches in the semi-lobotomized minion sweatshops and fantasy lands of the large corporations.

The voice of sanity and reason within whispers, at times, that is impossible to find unconditional happiness by sipping from the cup of illusion. It counsels that anything, unavailable now is not real, and therefore unworthy of our effort and investment. Nevertheless, all such whispers go unheeded, and those who prefer to temporize have already judged the present as incomplete. So they foolishly misguide themselves and believe they can build a better future without undertaking a complete overhaul and re-patterning of their entire process of thought. The present is interpreted, as lacking and defective given their current mind-state. So, they rationalize away the real cause of their pain and convince themselves that if they can keep that poker face going, the future will soon be glowing. All poor decisions and mistakes made prior are conceived of as random and unfortunate events that can easily be avoided moving forward. They conceive that wise decision-making is possible without undergoing any fundamental changes in themselves. This is nothing but magical thinking and the same an Alcoholic enlists, when he euphorically proclaims after three days sober, "*This time it will be different.*"

Sadly, a tiger does not change its stripes, and the underlying misery will remain and propagate unless one initiates substantial transformative innovations and thought reversals, in the present. All new experiences and opportunities will soon show how they are just new deceptive forms enclosing the same unhappy content. They may distract for a while, but the core unhappiness will again rear its head because the essential wrong-mindedness that underpins them has not changed an ounce.

Idol worship fuels itself on your imaginative capacities. Imagination, in turn, is the triggering catalyst that keeps your dream machine going. It enables you to bypass your present misery by substituting in an inspiring future. All that is needed is some fine-tuning, denial and mental juggling. Perhaps add a little more cunning, refinement and ingenuity into your cerebral suite. Imagination parades a feast of future images and glories which vitalize you and nourish the well of your spirit. Since it dazzles you with dreams of your incontestable specialness, you listen attentively to all it says. So begins your treasure hunt for the dream's chosen idols. One that never seems to end and you waste many lifetimes pursuing empty egocentric mirages in the desert. Without the spellbinding power of your imagination, your present state of misery could never be denied. This critical insight accommodates your release because pain becomes vanquished by your willingness to face it. Reality has never been elusive, but you have been absent from the present. The Real has become lost in the mists because of the endless series of idol chasing adventures and charades; you repeatedly engage in. You sold all for a dream of specialness. Sadly, even a serial killer plays that game and craves notoriety more than life itself. When all dreams fade, and all your hopes have been snuffed out, you will find your one true Home right in front of your eyes. Simply drop all foolish desires, fueled by your imagination, and you will find your place of rest. That genuine peace, you vainly sought, indulging elusive fantasies of the mind.

Extracting lasting satisfaction from hallucinations is impossible. Authentic peace and bliss are only ever be found in the present. They cannot be purchased from the future nor the past but are the natural consequence of a reintegrated and healed mind. A torn, disturbed and turbulent mind is not a valid receptacle for the Real to enter. How can a self, that is endlessly agitated and conflicted recognize and embrace the gifts of the Eternal? It is like water flowing through pebbles. The pebbles are not unified enough to prevent the water from trickling through them. So it is with all fragmented souls before Truth! Truth surrounds you, but your lack of understanding and integration makes you incapable of receiving its benediction. An illusion cannot hold the gifts of the Eternal. These gifts are always *Here-Now*, but you are not! You are engaged elsewhere—maybe on your smartphone or nose-diving into your laptop.

The most your fragmented self can accomplish is to borrow illusions of satisfaction in time. It is this; your imagination does! Nonetheless, all illusory satisfactions will invite an equal amount of grievances and discontent. The Course says that *"It is impossible to seek for pleasure through the body and not find pain." [ACIM, T-19.IV.B.12:1]* This is truly a lion's roar, and once again, we feel that crashing sword of wisdom upon our backs. An uncompromising sagacity and perspicacity, sufficiently generalized, to account for all circumstances and pursuits, in which we vainly mine for pleasure through the body. It does not bother to delve into specific examples. It does not empha-size, for instance, the futility of imbibing a particular con-coction, to achieve a total mellow high while avoiding oth-ers to restrain our inner demons. This self-contained in-sight declares the absolute impossibility of ever gaining any lasting contentment from any idol or illusion, centered on the body. All remain mirages in the desert that are powerless to quench your thirst. They keep you traveling through a bleak landscape where no satisfactions exist. Voyaging through the dream of time and separation your awareness becomes screened to those crucial, pivotal in-sights which confer genuine peace. Time and the belief in separation are codependent illusions, and together they establish an artificial framework for various deceptions to kick in. Thus they provide the fertile ground where all idols flourish.

HELL AND THE RELATIVE EXISTENCE

"This Earth, Disciple, is the Hall of Sorrow, wherein are set along the Path of dire probations, traps to ensnare thy EGO by the delusion called "Great Heresy."

['The Voice of the Silence]

One day you will wake up sweating, only to discover your life has been an absolute forgery. That day will expose your paper mache existence for the facsimile of ennui and mundanity, that it is. The delinquents on skid row got up to far more mischief and were veritably throbbing with life in comparison. You learned nothing, gained nothing, accomplished nothing. Instead, you dragged your way kicking and screaming through that proverbial *"unexamined life, not worth having."* All your days, you carelessly wasted as some chicken little, or lickspittle, not worth a fraction of a nickel. You are a mockery of humanity, a humiliation to the Cro-magnon species. Now as some palliated, etiolated ghost stuck in the mirror of existence, certain suffocating thoughts rise to haunt you. All you can do is swim about in that cesspool of lukewarm urine you have been spraying out, for a lifetime. You have no hope left, except to cower and cringe in mortal terror and wait for that lightning strike or death ray to strike from the heavens which finally incinerates your bovine ass, from the face of the earth.

We hover through this hallway of deception where we are content to remain as an illusion that mocks our former glory. It is a bleak and deserted corridor, impregnated with the obscuring haze of mysterious presences, and terrifying images. All becomes summoned into our perception through our wishfulness. Our inner lamp holds an Aladdin, who is ready to give us all that we desire. Sadly, we demand the wrong things and are easily bewitched and enchanted by lackluster offerings, in forms that seem pleasing. Hypnotized by our complicity to this delusion, we retain a deeply ingrained identification with the world of our senses. A multiplicity of false thought-forms parades before us that hijacks our attention. Never looking beyond these magician's tricks, we plunge into inescapable bondage to this dreamworld. Even so, we can never succeed in making the unreal, real and this Relative World will always remain powerless to reach to Truth. As the Course teaches:

"The unreal world *is* a thing of despair,
for it can never be."

[ACIM, T-12.VIII.7:8]

This hell we perceive is only an appearance—a nasty reflection, representative of our beliefs. It arose over time from all our desires, attachments and fears and is shaped to suit all our special needs, vile purposes, tastes, idiosyncrasies, predispositions, conceptual understandings and so forth. The Samskaras of our conditioned thought patterns crystallize into the concrete world, we perceive. It is elicited from an infinite set of possibilities, and it is perfectly adjusted to meet all our ideations and learning needs. Desire creates our future and fear weighs down on us with the burden of the past. Both obscure the radiance of the present moment. So truth becomes lost beneath the wild, delirious distortions of our split-mind! Caught in a perpetual state of confusion, we are unable to communicate the real. So, we fumble and hallucinate images that veil Reality! In the final analysis, what difference does it make, if we apotheosize ourselves into Gods in our mind-generated hallucination? What merit can we ever gain from ruling in a private kingdom entirely cut off from Truth? Hallucinations imprison, and turn each into a reactionary victim of their endogenous thought.

Since this unreal universe is born from erroneous thought, it is impotent to release us. It merely infiltrates our mind with numerous idiotic, relativistic notions, not worth a damn. Truth is not denigrated, nor usurped by the relative, but liberation must come from within ourselves. The Heavenly paradise will reemerge from our mental haze once all errors and apparent contradictions, are successfully resolved. Then the ensnaring web of the illusory will haunt us no more. As fear reinforces Hell, unconditional Love has the power to restore Heaven, back into our awareness.

Our hell has always been constructed from the arbitrary projections of our split-mind just as Heaven returns through extending the perfect understanding of Whole-Mind. Hell, depends intimately on time to perpetuate its illusion while Heaven knows only the timeless! Heaven and Hell are mutually exclusive kingdoms, and the presence of one causes us to lose awareness of the other. Hell is constructed from our private thoughts and wishful thinking while Heaven holds only the shared ideas of Universal Mind.

Hell only appeared when the great sleep descended upon Adam. Even so, it remains an imaginary world fabricated from false ideas. Regrettably, most cannot peer beyond this veil; and only a few have ever awoken. The rest remain trapped in the darkness of their distortions and then project this outward. Suffering a loss of vision, they can no longer appreciate anything for its inherent perfection. Time is that illusory medium in which opposing thoughts can be upheld, without their inherent contradictory nature ever becoming revealed. Such conflicts, we cannot rectify if we continue to choose the ego as your guide. They only arise because fundamental understandings have first been obscured, through denial. Time is that medium in which the real and unreal can appear to meet without either being able to knock the other out. It is only because of our profound state of internal chaos and confusion that Truth seems fragmented into a gazillion different pieces. These discombobulated pieces now seem to possess no meaningful relationships.

We each experience our existence through the illusion of Split-mind, and this we maintain through the dynamics of denial and projection. Since split-mind is incapable of apprehending the real, it sees its salvation in specialness. This unholy wish then compels us to make countless judgments and unjust evaluations because we need hierarchies of worth and value, to maintain our myths of specialness. Because of this recidivous ego desire, each aspect of Mind roams about feeling alienated, disconnected and isolated from its Source. Most spend their entire lives spellbound and hypnotized by a host of magical beliefs, which possess no intrinsic merit. They live empty lives, devoid of all clarity, understanding, meaningful purpose and hope. Each desperately tries to complete himself, by old-school methods, already proven to fail. Eventually, they become disenchanted and begin to scapegoat the world as the cause of their endless misery and failures. They never recognize that the tangled web of their misconceptions, inadequacies, biases, and weaknesses are the critical elements that obstruct their understanding.

Broken and spiritually decimated, they take this dark, despairing Haven as their home and undergo a psychological metamorphosis of disinformation and brainwashing that only imprisons further. Assimilating worthless ideas to sustain themselves, they are thrown about by an object-orientated luniverse, seemingly outside themselves. So do they fall hook, line, and sinker in the great slimy pools of self-induced deception! The veracity of which they take beyond all question. It is not long before the gods of positivism rise to become embraced and glorified. Few exit this illusionary artifice in which space, time and bodies forever intermingle and congeal into that amorphous blob known as perception. It is a hopeless depot where millions of illusions spring every moment to incapacitate and deceive. What are these gods of positivism, but those of Science, Technology, Cosmology, Economics, Modern Medicine and the like! Have they any power to save us—I think not! The evidence of ongoing human misery, famines wars, mysterious new diseases and the escalation of cycles of random violence demonstrate very cogently that positivism does not work. Where is the underlying essence in this dizzying convoluted fabric of illusions? Ultimately all self-made hells are spun from our belief in separation and reflect ego patterns of magical solution at their core.

North America is the golden palace where these gods incarnate in their most psychedelic forms. They grant special favors to all mindless surrogates willing to become termites on the mound of a materialistic universe. All those, ready to become sacrificed and consumed in the bonfire of earthly passions. Yes, you too can enjoy a high standard of living and free yourself from slavery to the farm. The paradise of plenty and a debt-free existence lies just up ahead. In the meantime, the treadmill calls and big government wants to pull all your strings and snoop around in your glory hole! Big pharma too, is getting ready to prey on your body and sell you on a lifetime of sickness. It aims to have you firmly hooked so that it can lend your life back to you with interest. Maybe you can just go for that jog through a vertiginous maze of serial killers, rogue bombers, and mass suicide cults while stepping over some tramp or opioid addict on the way to the store. Only to be then hit with some frivolous litigation, on your return. In every cubbyhole, the powers of justice have sent out their pigs to exercise political muscle. The goal is mass control and the elimination of all civil liberties from the face of the earth. All is carefully orchestrated and rigged by those oligarchical dictatorships that of course have our best interests at heart.

The shiny surface you perceive just reflects the superficial gloss over your deeper hell. The physical aspect arises from your firm commitment and belief in the body. The psychological is far more subtle and not so easily detected. It derives its immense influence from that unholy triad of sin, guilt, and fear. Sin maintains past time, guilt shrouds the real present, and fear unleashes its projections into an unwritten future. Thus do you become condemned to a repository of erroneous beliefs and the unreal entity known as the ego. The body is the chosen home and vehicle through which the ego flourishes. Just like any savvy master and commander, it uses this barrier and its dreams of specialness to inhibit and limit all genuine, empathic and meaningful communication.

It was only in our pre-fall condition that we experienced revelatory communications, which were perfectly pure, clear and unambiguous. Then we operated solely out of Whole-Mind, which is incapable of any distortion. All that ended, however, once the ego rose to prominence in our minds. Initiating communication failures is the ego's reactionary attempt to protect itself, for it exists in extreme fear of that which lies forever beyond its knowledge-base. In its panic, it tries to convince each that they are entombed behind a rapidly decaying wall of flesh. Recognizing, that some offering is needed, to elicit your support, it presents to you that tawdry, rust-filled gift of worldly idols. In particular, it tempts with the idol of your specialness. Through this, it hopes to dazzle or ensnare you into accepting its worldview.

Idols are poor substitutes for the real. You cannot know your innate wholeness while entertaining fantasies of the unreal. No idol has any real gift to give, but they parade before you in numerous tantalizing forms. They are represented by the objects or achievements which you venerate or esteem and by those exceptional individuals whom you place on your pedestal. Through idols, you seek to externalize the deeper cause of your misery. And so you project the source of salvation, satiation, and cure to this "outer" proxy. This strategy, however, can only be an exercise in displacement and it sends you careening rapidly in the wrong direction. On this misadventure, you expend enormous energy and time chasing the hallucinatory effects spawned from your mind. Having projected the source of completion outside yourself, you cannot avoid amplifying and distorting aspects of your perception to enhance the glory of your chosen idol. Somehow, you must have accepted yourself as unworthy and incomplete, to deem any idol sacred. Now it holds enormous sway over your thought, and it infuses your veins with its negative energy and destructive patterns. You are likely to become outright vicious, to protect it and will bathe in the victim mentality whenever its gifts are withheld. Doing so, you lose all mastery over your life.

Idols are the ego's surrogates for Reality. The life-saving water, they promise, always seems some distance away—a future prospect never to be tasted, "Now." Each of us cherishes a multitude of idols, in any given lifetime, and their fleeting chimerical nature reflects the ongoing evolutionary changes in our desires. No idol can satisfy the mind, nor can it quench our real thirst. None can connect us to spirit. Any attempt to complete ourselves on the "outside" must always fail. As we approach each, we recognize their healing water was a fantasy or myth we projected, into a form that attracted. Lack of awareness of our unassailable wholeness is the only lack. For this reason, all idols offer us death because retaining a belief in lack, denies our underlying divinity which leads to death. Whole-Mind makes no senseless journeys; It esteems not the transient and evanescent but rests securely, in its perfect understanding. Knowing all, it possesses all, and so it is entirely disinterested in pursuing idle phantoms of the mind.

AUTHOR BIO

Sharon Moriarty is a Mystic and Adventurer. In her past lives, she engaged professionally in Hardware Engineering, Management, Lecturing, Software Development, and Sales. She enjoys sharing her insights and wisdom on the Course material and communicating its ideas in a very lucid and in-depth manner. She hopes you enjoy your Spiritual journey.

Other Books by Sharon Moriarty

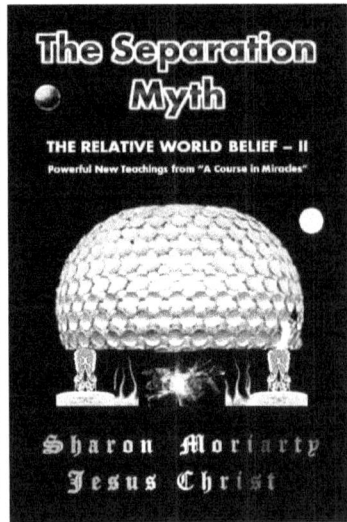

E-Books and Paperbacks Available now on Amazon and CreateSpace.

http://www.Amazon.com

A BRIEF HISTORY OF FEAR

The Relative World Belief – III

POWERFUL NEW TEACHINGS FROM

"A Course In Miracles"

Copyright © 2017 Sharon Moriarty

ISBN (Paperback): 978-0-9971179-6-7

Library of Congress Control Number (LCCN): 2017912037

GATEWAY TO ETERNITY PUBLICATIONS

http://www.GatewayToEternity.com